WESTERNS

It is a common assertion that the history of America is written in its Westerns, but how true is this?

In this guidebook, John White discusses the evolution of the Western through history and looks at theoretical and critical approaches to Westerns such as genre analysis, semiotics, representation, ideology, discourse analysis, narrative, realism, auteur and star theory, psychoanalytical theory, postmodernism, and audience response. The book includes case studies of eight key Westerns:

- Stagecoach
- My Darling Clementine
- Shane
- The Good, The Bad, and the Ugly
- McCabe and Mrs. Miller
- Unforgiven
- Brokeback Mountain
- The Assassination of Jesse James by the Coward, Robert Ford

Including a chronology of significant events for the Western genre, a glossary and further reading, this introduction to an important genre in film studies is a great guide for students.

John White is lecturer in Film and Media at Anglia Ruskin University, UK. He is also an A-level examiner for Film Studies with the WJEC and a teacher of Film, English ⬚⬚⬚⬚⬚ ⬚⬚⬚⬚ Community College. He is co-author of AS Film Studies: ⬚⬚⬚⬚⬚⬚⬚⬚ ⬚⬚⬚ ⬚8) and A2 Film Studies: The Essential Intro⬚ ⬚⬚⬚⬚⬚ r of 50 Key British Films (2008) and 50 ⬚⬚⬚⬚⬚

D1145572

Routledge Film Guidebooks

The Routledge Film Guidebooks offer a clear introduction to and overview of the work of key filmmakers, movements, or genres. Each guidebook contains an introduction, including a brief history; defining characteristics and major films; a chronology; key debates surrounding filmmakers, movements, or genres; and pivotal scenes, focusing on narrative structure, camerawork, and production quality.

Bollywood: A Guidebook to
Popular Hindi Cinema
Tejaswini Ganti

James Cameron
Alexandra Keller

Jane Campion
Deb Verhoeven

Horror
Brigid Cherry

Film Noir
Jennifer Fay and Justus Nieland

Documentary
Dave Saunders

Romantic Comedy
Claire Mortimer

Westerns
John White

WESTERNS

JOHN WHITE

Routledge
Taylor & Francis Group

LONDON AND NEW YORK

First edition published 2011
by Routledge
2 Park Square, Milton Park, Abingdon, Oxon OX14 4RN

Simultaneously published in the USA and Canada
by Routledge
270 Madison Ave, New York, NY 10016

Routledge is an imprint of the Taylor & Francis Group, an informa business

Typeset in Joanna by
HWA Text and Data Management, London
Printed and bound in Great Britain by
CPI Antony Rowe, Chippenham, Wiltshire

British Library Cataloguing in Publication Data
A catalogue record for this book is available from the British Library

Library of Congress Cataloging in Publication Data
White, John, 1956–
    Westerns / John White.
        p. cm. – (Routledge film guidebooks)
    Includes bibliographical references and index.
    1. Western films – United States – History and criticism.
    I. Title.
    PN1995.9.W4W495 2010
    791.436′278–dc22   2010024811

ISBN 13: 978-0-415-55812-9 (hbk)
ISBN 13: 978-0-415-55813-6 (pbk)
ISBN 13: 978-0-203-83531-9 (ebk)

CONTENTS

LIST OF FIGURES

ACKNOWLEDGEMENTS

I am grateful to Aileen Storry at Routledge for her constant support and to John Walsh for his technical help.

1

INTRODUCTION

THE APPROACH OF THIS BOOK

This book aims to provide readers with an overview of a genre that is frequently viewed and written about with enthusiasm but which is less often seen in relation to the range of possible analytical approaches offered by film theory. The main focus will be on introducing readers to a variety of theoretical approaches that could be adopted when studying the Western. Books on Westerns can devote much of their space to retelling the story found in each film under discussion: here, by contrast, it will be assumed readers are already familiar with the basic plot and are ready to begin considering potential ways of understanding the film in relation to the culture and society that has produced it.

It is a common assertion that the central myth of the United States is written in its Westerns, and there is clearly considerable truth in this statement.[1] However, in books on the subject, the investigation of this myth often amounts to little more than a retelling of legendary stories of the 'Wild West.' This approach tends to consider only the obvious surface narrative exchanges found in the films; struggles between groups such as cattle barons and 'sod-busters,' cavalry and 'Indians,' and marshals and 'hired-guns.' In places, the genre is more deeply examined in relation to the history of the period in which the films have been made, with the relevance of both American foreign and domestic policies being considered. This approach offers profounder insights into the Western and will form part of the analysis on offer here.[2] It will involve some consideration of the class confrontations, racial antagonisms, national identity crises, generational dislocations, gender tensions, and sexual repressions found within Westerns and the apparent certainties advanced around these issues. It will be suggested that each of these elements needs to be viewed as existing in relation to both the historical period represented in the film and the era within which the film has been produced. Westerns tend to take as their subject matter a particular (if somewhat elastic) historical era, but they also reflect (and participate in) the various contexts of the periods in which they have been made.

The danger with an approach such as this is that it can lead to rather vague generalized responses to individual films. For example, we may simply see Hollywood Westerns of the late 1960s as reflecting the involvement of the United States in the Vietnam War and those from the previous 20 years as commenting on the Cold War.[3] There is certainly some truth in such linking of Westerns to the historical period of their birth, but the detail needs to be considered carefully in relation to each film with an awareness that it is just as certain there are other equally interesting things that could be said about these same films. For this reason, a range of theoretical approaches will be explored in relation to Westerns. The effort will be to demonstrate ways in which further dimensions to each film can be uncovered and to suggest that the most fruitful investigations will often involve a combination of approaches. The best that can be hoped for in such a short book dealing with such a vast potential collection of films is that possible forms of investigation will be made sufficiently clear for readers to take these forward for themselves in the analysis of further Westerns.

As we are dealing with a commonly recognized genre, genre analysis will provide a starting point for our theoretical consideration of Westerns. As a genre, Westerns display a series of common features over time: recurring reworked visions of landscape and settled place, continually re-emerging set types of character confrontation, and constantly re-examined thematic oppositions. Westerns explore features of human experience that have remained constant: the isolation of the individual, the potential brutality of group and individual human interaction, the willingness of human beings to journey in search of a 'better' life, the tensions of family relationships, and the harshness of the natural world. Some of these features, and others that might be said to establish the Western as a genre, will be explored and outlined in relation to specific films. Ultimately, however, the limitations of both the generalized historical approach, mentioned earlier, and the simplistic categorization frequently associated with genre analysis will be identified. Against these shortcomings, this book aims to assert the potential insights offered by a range of further theoretical explorations and proposes the usefulness of incorporating a range of approaches within any analysis of a specific text. A complex matrix of films fall within the category of Westerns and each should be dealt with as a specific text existing within specific contexts and investigated from clearly designated theoretical standpoints. It is at this point, as a range of theoretical perspectives are employed to examine the features of a particular film (or particular films) made at a particular time (and, therefore, within specific contexts), that the genre approach and the historical approach can return to validity.

It is worth noting that, although this book will focus on Westerns, readers should be able to take the outlined theoretical approaches on offer and apply them to further film genres of their own choice. Although the debate over the nature, place, and role of genre analysis within film studies is not directly addressed, the clear implication of the line being taken here is that such analysis must take place in unison with other possibilities. The film text is situated within a series of overlapping and intertwined contexts involving historical, ideological, social, and economic considerations; is part of a process of production and consumption; is received in popular and critical terms; and becomes implicated in the development of theoretical discourses. The resulting polysemic nature of the text naturally creates a polysemy of theoretical and interpretative possibilities. Despite the fact that distinctive choices of approach to particular films will continually be made within this book, this underlying fact remains, and it should, therefore, be taken as understood that an array of further possibilities of investigation for any single text or combination of texts will remain unexplored. Any textual analysis we might undertake is forever coming into being and is never fully formed: an existentialist choice of possibilities continually exists.

AN INTRODUCTORY APPROACH TO WESTERNS

Westerns exist within the context of a Hollywood cinema industry that has operated as part of both the 'American' domestic economy and the global economy since before the First World War. These films also take their place within the wider media, specifically within a popular culture of frontier-town newspapers, serial magazines, paperback novellas, Wild West shows, radio shows, and TV series. At the same time, all of this – the cinema industry and the extended media culture – has taken its place within a changing twentieth-century society while putting forward representations of (in particular, but not exclusively) nineteenth-century American society. Westerns must, therefore, be seen in relation to the flux of American society over an extended period; that is, as existing at the moment of their production and exhibition within a pattern of institutions, types of socio-economic relationship, forms of organization, and socially created norms and values and referring to an earlier period with its own expression of these social dynamics.[4]

The nature of genres in general and the Western in particular will be examined in the opening section of Chapter 3 of this book through an examination of specific case-study films. The concept will be considered in terms of its everyday use and in relation to theoretical considerations such as iconography and audience expectations. However, some initial discussion of the concept of genre is necessary as this book takes as its most basic premise the existence of a group of films that readers are going to be prepared to see packaged together as forming in some way a distinctive category of (in particular, but not exclusively) Hollywood movies. Briefly, the rules and conventions of genre are said to constitute a type of language, or code, by which filmmakers construct film while at the same time operating as a language, or code, by which audiences read film. These rules and conventions are seen as being subject to change over time as social outlooks (and audiences) alter and filmmakers develop the genre.

This concept of genre enables us to theorize about the ways in which films are organized. We are able to consider codes (systems of signs communicating meanings) and conventions (shared cultural, social, and textual practices) both within and between films. It is these codes and conventions and our familiarity with them that make it possible for us to 'read,' or understand, films. However, although the codes and conventions of a genre may come to seem to be so, they are not 'natural.' Through codes and conventions that are agreed between producers and audiences, a Western from the 1940s, for example, presents us with a very particular version of maleness. Over time, social norms and expectations change, and so conventions displayed in textual practice change. In our example, the nature of 'maleness' might come to be questioned or, diverging further, former notions of maleness might be satirized. A genre has the flexibility to incorporate such change while retaining a sense of itself as a continuing, coherent (if evolving) type of cultural expression.

In general terms, genres such as Westerns have been seen, on the one hand, as operating as a ritualistic playing out of social issues for the audience and, on the other, as a presentation of ideological positions for the audience's consumption. Ultimately, however, genre can exist only within the relationship of particular spectators to specific films at certain moments. Genre has to be seen in relation to the expectations viewers bring to films and uses to which they put films (Altman, 1999). This is not to say broader cultural and ideological factors are not at stake and that genre as a social fact does not exist outside of the viewing experience but that the crucial motivating dynamic of genre exists in the interface between spectator and screen.

Despite this core moment of active agency, it is acknowledged here from the outset that the concept of genre also helps the film industry to manufacture products that are known to be acceptable to audiences, targeting particular market segments and tailoring the product to evolving social norms and expectations. In this way, audiences, as consumers, are able to organize their viewing, attending the cinema (or, more recently, buying DVDs or downloading films) to obtain the mix of genres they personally desire. It is also the case that within this process of production and consumption, genre enables advertisers to target their own market segments, or niche markets. Genres such as the Western, then, have provided one means of organizing the production, distribution, and exhibition of films as commercial products and facilitating the parallel consumption of further associated merchandised products.

Defining the exact extent and nature of the genre of Westerns is more problematic. Delineating boundaries in terms of the historical date the films are set (often 1840–1890 is used) or the place in which the stories take place (the American West) is not just fraught with difficulties, it is ultimately impossible. Why not 1830, or 1900, or contemporary to the date of production as with B-Westerns in the 1930s? What exactly are the dimensions of the American West? How far to the north or south does it stretch? Can we have Westerns employing locations east of the Mississippi? Similarly, bounding the Western in terms of content, film style, and generic purity is equally difficult. A considerable variety of costumes, props, and locations have proved possible; certain narrative structures have recurred but not in such a way as to exclude other possible constructions; some types of shot have been used in a whole series of Westerns but not in such a way as to be an unavoidable requirement of the genre; and, frequently generic hybridity has proved the very lifeblood of the genre. Genres are fluid, plastic, dynamic, used in different ways by different critics at different times for different purposes. However, though this means the term does not have ultimate, finally fully determinable parameters, it does not mean the term has not had potent cultural meaning for filmmakers, the film industry, audiences, critics, and scholars over a period of 100 years. Categorizing elements of the world around us is functionally useful in a variety of ways but never finally sustainable in terms of providing us with hermetically sealed groupings. If we define the Western in terms of similarity of plot or storyline, we find ourselves outlining and allowing genre membership to a series of deviations from whatever we posit as the 'classic' structure. If we define our genre according to iconography, we find ourselves with an ever-lengthening list of modifications to the stereotypical cowboy hat, six-gun, and horse. If we define our genre according to subject matter, we may force most films into cycles involving pioneering wagon trains, cavalry–Indian engagements, law and order in Frontier towns, homesteaders versus cattle ranchers, and Civil War–related material, but then we are faced with defining what might be seen as linking such an array of cycles. What could be said to make such a range of subject matter coherent as a single genre?

Christian Metz suggested a genre could be seen as 'a single vast and continuous text' with its own 'textual system' (Metz, 1974: 121–126). Films within a genre such as the Western are seen as having recurring cultural codes, themes, and ritual events such as male friendship and the gunfight and cinematic codes such as the *mise en scène* of the frontier town. This may be, as suggested earlier, ultimately unsustainable[5] but it remains a useful approach to Westerns. Similarly, Claude Levi-Strauss's concept of 'myths' as a means by which cultures organize their view of the world into a structure of basic oppositions remains helpful. Jim Kitses employs this as a starting point for constructing an elaborate system of oppositional ideas to be found in Westerns centring on the 'freedom' of 'the individual' set against the 'restriction' offered by 'the community,' the 'purity' but potential 'savagery' of 'nature' set against the 'corruption' of 'culture,' and the values of 'the West' set against the values of 'the East.' He suggests all of these oppositions stem from a fundamental tension between the concepts of 'wilderness' and 'civilization' which overarches everything else (Kitses, 1969). What Kitses provides us with is not so much a necessary, unavoidable structure for the Western but a description of what we tend to find in Westerns. Even so, his schematic representation of the genre remains highly suggestive of an entire series of interesting interplays of ideas that occur in the Western and a valuable aid to discussing these ideas. In the end, to search for a meta-structure, a meta-narrative, or a meta-form for the Western is to quest for the unobtainable: categorizing as an activity does not work in terms of finality. And yet, the theory-based effort to 'nail down' the Western continually offers fruitful moments of insight. Kitses's use of the term *civilization*, it might be argued, should in fact be 'American civilization,' that peculiar creation of an amalgam between pioneering independence and something that might be denoted 'neighbourliness' as opposed to 'community.' His use of 'individual' and 'community,' it might be argued, omits important related concepts of 'hordes' and 'the mob.' However, such arguments merely contribute toward pointing up the rewarding layers of discussion such structuralist frameworks can provide.

Will Wright (1975) considers four basic plots for Westerns: the classic plot of a stranger arriving in town and restoring order; a version of this plot in which the hero comes from within the community; a vengeance plot with a central character seeking revenge; and a professional plot centring on paid gunfighters. All four plots might be said to focus upon the failure of community and the bringing about of some form of natural justice. Wright identifies four fundamental oppositions – exterior–interior, good–evil, strong–weak, and wild–civilized – but at least the first three of these, and usually some version of the fourth, can be found in all manner of films. Again, we have a useful foray into understand something of the key ideas at work within Westerns but, again, we need to bear in mind that in selecting certain Westerns patterns constructed after the event can always be made to fit the 'evidence.'

There is no final, specific formula that constitutes the Western: in common with all other genres, the Western has at its disposal a constantly evolving repository of subject matter, stylistic flourishes, and narrative structures. 'Reflexivity,' that is, the way in which new films respond to examples of the genre that have gone before, is not a post-1960 feature of the Western but something that has always taken place. The supposed 'classic' Western, *Stagecoach* (John Ford, 1939), exists in clear relation not only to B-movies from the 1930s but to the ideas and forms of representation to be found in earlier silent Westerns. The term *Western* comes into increasing use in relation to film during the later part of the silent period but, even before this, films focusing on subject matter based in the West clearly existed in relation to an ongoing American cultural mining of the concept of the West as a place of frontier confrontations.

NOTES

1. 'It (the Western) was,' as Peter Bogdanovich said, 'the essential American myth,' and that myth had started long before the cinema came along to exploit it. It had originated in the dime novels and pulp fiction – the works of Ned Buntline and the like – that had begun to appear in the 1860s, in the paintings of Frederic Remington and Charles M. Russell, and the thriving Wild West shows (notably Buffalo Bill Cody's) of the Victorian era' (Norman, 1991: 252).

2. See, for example, Corkin, 2004.

3. ' ... in the rhetoric of the antiwar movement, the war was by the middle 1960s being redrawn as an exact reversal of the western, one in which a pastoral people were being subjected to the onslaught of a European-like empire. By the end of the decade, the western itself had been largely supplanted by such 'Vietnam westerns' or 'anti-westerns' as *Soldier Blue* (1970) and *Little Big Man* (1971); by the end of the Vietnam era, it had virtually disappeared' (Anderegg, 1991: 143).

4. The term *culture* should be considered carefully in relation to the Western, particularly in terms of the ways in which popular culture has been theorized as an area of exchange and as an arena of contestation between classes and ideologies. (See, for example, Fiske, 1989.)

5. Vast panoramic shots may be found in a fair range of Westerns, but their absence would not debar a film from the genre. Similarly, rapid traveling shots may be employed frequently, but 'the chase' is not exclusive to Westerns.

2

THE EVOLUTION OF THE WESTERN

SILENT 'WESTERNS'

Some of the features that are to become key narrative elements of the genre are to be found in early silent Westerns from the late 1890s and early 1900s.[1] Minute-long films such as *Cripple Creek Bar-Room Scene*[2] and *Poker at Dawson City* (both 1899) from Thomas Edison's Manufacturing Company show card-playing, heavy-drinking saloon scenes. Actualities such as *Cattle Fording Stream* and *Lassoing a Steer* (both 1898, Edison) display a fascination with the life of the cowboy. Further short films such as *Sioux Ghost Dance* and *Buffalo Dance* (both 1894, Edison) and *Serving Rations to the Indians* (1898, Edison) display an interest in but also mixed attitudes toward Native Americans as an ethnic group.

> Indians were no longer perceived as an overt threat, and a nostalgic image of the historical noble savage, the vanishing 'first' Americans, became increasingly popular.
>
> (Kilpatrick, 1999: 17)

Arrival of Train at Station (1903, American Mutoscope and Biograph) acknowledges the importance of the railroads in opening up the West.

Figure 2.1 Placing the audience in the firing line (*The Great Train Robbery*, 1903)

Western Stage Coach Hold Up (1904, Edison) examines the precursor of the train and focuses on the 'hold-up.' *Cowboy Justice* (G. W. Bitzer, 1904, Biograph) shows a gunfight and (even if unconvincingly) summary lynch-law justice. Edwin S. Porter's *The Great Train Robbery* (1903, Edison) begins the process of developing the robbery, the chase, and the shoot-out into an engaging narrative structure.

In films such as *The Redman and the Child* (D. W. Griffith, 1908, Biograph), an Indian exacts revenge in what will later become the classic role of the white Western hero. An initial comfortable relationship between an older white man, his grandson, and a Native American is destroyed by two white men who kill the older man and capture the young boy to find out where the Indian's gold is hidden. The returning 'redman' kills the white men and rescues the child. In *The Redman's View* and *The Indian Runner's Romance* (both D. W. Griffith, 1909, Biograph), the whites are again villains; in the first case, they are greedy for land and, in the second, gold. In *The Redman's View*, Indians are forced to leave their land in an episode that references an actual episode from Native American history, the Trail of Tears.[3] Using Biblical terminology the inter-titles describe it as 'The Exodus: The Long Trek.' Walking all the time, the Indians are continually moved on by white men with guns over harsh, rocky terrain with the chief symbolically dying along the way. Native

American actors, such as Elijah Tahamont ('Chief Dark Cloud') in *The Song of the Wildwood Flute* (D. W. Griffith, 1910, Biograph), have substantial roles in these early films. And, the end of a Native American way of life often seems to be presented as a sad regret. This is particularly suggested by shots of 'Indians' positioned alone and staring off into the distance as in *Comata, the Sioux* and *Leather Stocking* (both D. W. Griffith, 1909, Biograph).[4] The possibility of friendship between whites and Indians is frequently demonstrated. One of the closing shots of *Rose o'Salem-Town* (Griffith, 1910, Biograph), for example, shows a frontier trapper shaking hands with a Mohawk. Often, women are shown as the catalyst bringing the two ethnic groups together. In *A Redskin's Bravery* (1911, New York Motion Picture Company/Bison), the woman is explicitly shown as linking the two men in the final shot.[5] At the end of *White Fawn's Devotion* (James Young Deer, 1910, Pathe), a white settler is reunited with his Indian wife and their daughter while being watched over by the Native American community. Loving interracial marriage and peaceful coexistence seem to be at the thematic heart of the film.

By 1910, Westerns formed 20 percent of all U. S. films released. Around this time, the main studios began to move from New York and Chicago to West Coast locations, eventually congregating around Los Angeles and forming the basis for what was to become 'Hollywood.' This naturally produced a noticeable change in the dominant form of landscape used in the Western; directors and cinematographers filming on location were now faced with predominantly desert landscapes. Accompanying this shift in location there seems to have been a change in the dominant perspective taken toward Native Americans who moved from often being seen as 'noble' and loyal to being increasingly portrayed as uncivilized, brutal, and savage. One-to-one friendships between Indians and white men were a feature of silent films pre-1910 but, after this time, the 'Indians' tended to become an undifferentiated horde. The Plains Wars became the key historical backdrop for many of these films, with pioneering wagon trains, Indian war parties, and the U. S. Cavalry featuring heavily. In line with the racial stereotypes he adopted in his later *Birth of a Nation* (1915, D. W. Griffith Corporation/ Epoch Producing Corporation), D. W. Griffith portrays Indians as fawning in *In Old California* (1910, Biograph) and ready to attack white settlers without provocation in *The Twisted Trail* (1910, Biograph). In *The Battle of Elderbush Gulch* (1913, Biograph), a film that is an odd mixture of the light and the serious, Griffith shows an Indian murdering a child by dashing its brains out. In this film, settlers in a ranch house are about to be massacred when the cavalry rides to the rescue, playing out a further central scene for later Westerns.[6] As the Western develops in Hollywood, the harsh landscape that is available for location shooting is found to lend itself to the binary oppositions centring on barbarity versus civilization that become such a central facet of the genre.

The increasing level of violence in Westerns is reflected in titles such as *On the War Path* (Kenean Buel, 1911, Kalem) and *The Indian Massacre* (Francis Ford, 1912, New York Motion Picture Company/101-Bison). In Griffith's *The Massacre* (1912, Biograph), a more coherent piece of work than *Elderbush Gulch*, there are in fact two massacres, one of Indians and another of whites. Women and children are killed alongside men, and the only survivors of the final assault by the 'Indians' are a mother and her child found beneath the corpses of a 'Last Stand' that is clearly meant to echo that of Custer.[7] The violence of the Indians is for once given a source of motivation: an attack on their own village in which a mother and child are shown left among the dead. The white child is used by Griffith not simply as an occasion for melodrama but as a focus of innocence.

These films were seen at the time as being extremely realistic, but notions of realism are culturally and historically relative. The 'realism' being reflected here was largely the created realism of Wild West shows such as that of Buffalo Bill Cody, and the genre of Wild West art epitomized by the work of Frederic Remington. These two late-nineteenth-century cultural sources exerted key influences upon the popular understanding of history and, therefore, through audience expectation contributed toward shaping the movies that were made. *The Last Drop of Water* (Griffith, 1911, Biograph) shows a wagon train besieged by Indians and rescued by the arrival of the cavalry. *Fighting Blood* (Griffith, 1911, Biograph) shows the classic central Western character of the Civil War veteran preparing his family for the inevitable Indian attack. In narrative terms, this type of film offered a clear sense of good and evil for the audience. The climax was action-packed, the heroics required could be developed from film to film, and the resolution could be satisfying for the audience. The period focused around the Indian Wars was the most aggressively expansionist of the westward move into the interior of the continent. Now, in the 1910s, expansion was beginning abroad particularly into Central America and the Caribbean, what would become known as 'America's backyard,' and these films enabled a flag-waving nationalism to be displayed.[8] If the creation of empire, in the 'Interior' in the nineteenth century and in the Caribbean in the early twentieth century, was to be seen as an 'epic' venture, an appropriately epic landscape was an effective space within which to see this American 'destiny' being fulfilled. At the same time, white racial superiority was emphasized in tune with a strand of jingoistic political attitudes from the period most clearly expressed by Theodore Roosevelt.[9] Furthermore, from a cinematic perspective, the drama of movement through an expansive landscape was best captured through the speed of movement made possible by the introduction of cavalry (both U. S. and Indian) and the size offered by the wagon train. Car chases were beginning to make an appearance in other films, and Westerns needed to be able to match this form of projected excitement. So, the type of Westerns made in this decade was effective in both production and patriotic terms.

The connection between Wild West shows and Westerns of the period is made explicit in a series of films produced by Thomas Ince in Santa Monica, California for the New York Motion Picture Company. In *War on the Plains* (Thomas Ince, 1912, New York Motion Picture Company/101-Bison), ox-drawn wagons, 'pioneers' riding horses, and longhorn cattle from The Miller Brothers' 101 Ranch Real Wild West Show are 'attacked' by mounted Sioux warriors from the same show. In *Custer's Last Fight* (Ince/Ford, 1912, New York Motion Picture Company/101-Bison)[10] the same Sioux are used, as they are again in *The Invaders* (Ince/Ford, 1912, New York Motion Picture Company/Kay-Bee). In this last film, whites are brutally attacked, and the 7th Cavalry is massacred, but only after railroad bosses have broken a peace treaty in attempting to push a line through the Dakotas. Wild West shows used the fear-tinged thrill of being able to see, 'peepshow-like,' the threatening 'Other' to excite audiences. Here, Westerns were beginning to use the same approach. As a tribe, the Sioux offered a useful shorthand version of Native American for the movies. This group dressed distinctively, had a distinctively 'different' appearance, and led a nomadic unsettled existence. Every aspect of their culture was distinctively different from that of the white settlers. They rode horses but rode them bareback. They didn't want to settle but wanted to remain nomadic. They were hunters and not agriculturalists. They did not build towns with rows of houses but could move a wigwam-dotted village at a moment's notice. Other tribes would not be so easily and clearly delineated as Other but, if all Native Americans came to be seen in this mould, political issues became clear-cut.

The title, *The Invaders*, could be deemed ambiguous in that the invaders could be the Indians who are responsible for violent attacks against whites, and yet, any invasion that is occurring is clearly of Native American lands. The film's style, in its relative lack of editing and close-ups, documents the chaos of battle without producing audience identification with one side or the other. In the end, the besieged fort is relieved, the Indians are seen as savages, and the problematic Indian, Sky Star, who in falling in love with a white man has threatened the racial divide, conveniently dies. However, both the title and the narrative source of conflict as being white men breaking a treaty remain to unsettle any easy reading. Furthermore, the most attractive and the most challenging character in the film is Sky Star. She is an active, horse-riding, female character who challenges racial and (in choosing her suitor for herself) gender boundaries.

Cowboys, as played by William S. Hart, for example, were popular during the 1910s as the 'good-badman' (the man with a shady past who is redeemed by love), whereas others, as played by Tom Mix, for example, epitomized the Western action hero. The majority of Westerns made during the later silent period tended to be these 'low-brow,' low-budget films (a trend that continued through the '30s, '40s, and '50s before transferring into TV productions of the '60s), but some high-budget Westerns are also made in the 1920s, for example, *The Covered Wagon* (James Cruze, 1923, Paramount) and *The Iron Horse* (John Ford, 1924, Fox). These films try to endorse a particular version of history, giving their audience a sense of the pioneering spirit and inevitable march of progress seen to be at the heart of the opening up of the West and crucial to the sense of U. S. nationhood that needed to be established after the divisions of the Civil War. The most obvious thing to be said about Westerns from the silent period is that they are dealing with episodes from the relatively recent American past. If the genre has now become historical drama, it was then addressing experiences that remained very much within living memory.[11] Both William S. Hart and Tom Mix were at Wyatt Earp's funeral when he died in 1929, aged 80 (Barra, 2009: 340).

WESTERNS IN THE 1930s

During the 1930s, a series of A-Westerns make a conscious effort to present a particular interpretation of the history of the American West in the second half of the nineteenth century. Among these films are *The Big Trail* (Raoul Walsh 1930, Fox); *Billy the Kid* (King Vidor, 1930, MGM); *Cimarron* (Wesley Ruggles, 1931, RKO); *Annie Oakley* (George Stevens, 1935, RKO); *The Plainsman* (Cecil B. de Mille, 1936, Paramount); *Wells Fargo* (Frank Lloyd, 1937, Paramount); *Jesse James* (Henry King, 1939, 20th Century Fox); and *Dodge City* (Michael Curtiz, 1939, Warner Brothers). In their own way, each of these films attempts to celebrate the 'opening up' of the West. *The Big Trail*, for example, looks back to early pioneers taking the Oregon Trail in the 1840s[12] using a 70-mm wide-screen format to emphasize a sense of this as an epic venture. The spectacle provided by various imposing landscapes is one of the key components in this style of Western. *The Big Trail* is filmed in Sacramento, California to obtain the opening riverboat scenes, in Arizona for the desert scenes, in Utah and Wyoming for the rocky canyon scenes, in the Sierras in California for the snow scenes, and in the Sequoia National Park for the final scenes set among giant redwoods. In this way, it integrates each of the key landscapes and territories of the West within a single text. It also attempts to synthesize a vast, many-faceted political concept into a single powerful idea, giving expression to something too complex to be contained other than within the controlled tones of myth. The power, grandeur, beauty, and threat of the natural world is ever-present in a big-budget Western such as this and, often, Indians in their unmotivated, sudden, unexpected attacks can seem like just another threat from the natural world to be endured and overcome.

The opening title of *The Big Trail* is 'The Conquest of the West.' A later inter-title announces, 'The last outpost: the turning back place for the weak, the starting place for the strong.' This is very much in keeping with the attitudes expressed by Theodore Roosevelt.

> I wish to preach, not the doctrine of ignoble ease, but the doctrine of toil and effort, of labor and strife; to preach that highest form of success which comes, not to the man who desires mere easy peace, but to the man who does not shrink from danger, from hardship, or from bitter toil, and who out of these wins the splendid ultimate triumph.
>
> (Roosevelt, 2006: 1)

The attempt here is to create 'a tradition of honor, fair play, justice and democratic idealism' and 'a foundation myth for American culture' (Jewell, 2007: 198). However, with the Depression having an effect on audiences, A-Westerns lost money in the early '30s and were put on hold by studios until the second half of the decade.

The bulk of the genre in this period is B-Westerns (usually running less than 60 minutes) wherein the approach to both production and exhibition is entirely different. Edward Buscombe suggests there were just 44 A-Westerns made in the 1930s out of a total of more than 1,000 feature-length Westerns (Buscombe, 1991: 427–8). B-movies were made to be shown as support films rather than main features, were extremely low budget, and were often shot in a matter of days. On the surface, they show little obvious interest in the history of the West, but each is underpinned by a belief that the assumed Western ideals of fair play, honor, and justice are fundamentally American and are to be upheld by the hero. This is particularly so in the films made by the most famous B-Western cowboy actors of the period, William Boyd and Gene Autry. Boyd played the character of the good cowboy 'Hopalong' Cassidy in more than 60 films through the late 1930s and the 1940s, most of which were released through Paramount. Gene Autry, 'The Singing Cowboy,' made more than 40 Westerns in the 1930s with Republic and a few more after the war with Columbia. The career of Roy Rogers, another clean-cut singing cowboy, also began in the late 1930s. In 1939, he made nine short Westerns for Republic with the same director, Joseph Kane, and with George 'Gabby' Hayes as his side-kick in several of them. Some B-Westerns, such as *New Frontier* (Carl Pierson, 1935, Republic), which is set during the Oklahoma land rush of 1889 but has outlaws who are desperate for food and trail scouts who face unemployment, would seem to reflect the social realities of the contemporary period of the 1930s. *Wyoming Outlaw* (George Sherman, 1939, Republic) suggests fluctuations in the demand for wheat after 1918 led to some farmers' being ruined. One character here defends poaching by suggesting people's hunger should be set above the law. Often, the Old West (or, more correctly, a particular concept of the Old West) seems to exist alongside a new era in these films, and always the modern period is shown as having something to learn from the values and attitudes of the 'old days.' Despite the presence of automobiles and telephones, the central protagonist, played by John Wayne in these last two films, inevitably rides a horse and brings honesty, integrity, and justice in his saddlebags. The use of the Western formula centred on the upright hero is never stronger than in these serial-style movies in this period. In *Days of Jesse James* (Joseph Kane, 1939, Republic), Roy Rogers plays the same essential role. This film is made 10 years after the Wall Street Crash, but the central element of the plot is a corrupt banker who organizes a raid on his own bank, enabling Gabby Hayes to pronounce, 'Let me tell you something, young fella. Never have nothing to do with no banks.'[13]

The Telegraph Trail (Tenny Wright, 1933, Warner Brothers) is unusual for B-Westerns in that it focuses on the struggle against Indians. The tenor of this film is more in line with the retelling of history found in A-Westerns. The opening text sets the scene: 'For many years, against tremendous odds, American civilization struggled slowly Westward: 1830 The Covered Wagon, 1840 The Stage Coach, 1850 The Pony Express, 1860 The First Telegraph.' The film concludes with the classic circled wagons being defended against an Indian attack and the cavalry riding to the rescue. More typical was a film such as *Riders of Destiny* (Robert N. Bradbury, 1933, Monogram/Lone Star Productions) in which Wayne plays Singin' Sandy Saunders,[14] an agent sent from Washington to deal with a crooked local businessman. In such films, the audience is encouraged to see the government as the savior of ordinary rural communities. Certainly the film would seem to relate to actual conditions during the period. The early 1930s was the period of the 'Dust Bowl' in Oklahoma, Texas, New Mexico, Colorado, and Kansas, when drought dried the soils of the plains and high winds blew it away in huge dust clouds. In the film, the community is facing severe drought, with the Kincaid Land and Water Company cutting off their water supply. One woman advocates giving up. 'Your cattle are dying. Your crops are withering. You're fighting a hopeless fight,' she tells the men. After fistfights, gunfights, and dramatic chases, Wayne, of course, puts things right, releasing a torrent of water into the valley. There then follows a lengthy sequence showing children and adults playing in the water and livestock happily taking to the water. This film is released early in the 1930s, but the drought and consequent dust storms (on occasions darkening skies all the way to the Atlantic) continued throughout the decade. Film may here, as so often, be offering an escapist fantasy, but it was a release from hardship those worst affected would not have had the spare cash to have enjoyed.[15]

Small teams of filmmakers and actors would work on these B-Westerns, producing them (as Buscombe's research shows, see earlier) at a prodigious rate. Lone Star productions in the early 1930s often had Robert N. Bradbury as writer and director, Archie Stout as director of photography, Carl Pierson as editor (later also a director), Wayne as the leading character, and stuntman Yakima Canutt somewhere in the cast. Using units of workers in this way was a feature of the Hollywood studio system, allowing for increased efficiency. The stunts were a vital component of the entertainment: straightforward fistfights and horse chases, fights on moving wagons, horse stunts such as riders jumping off cliffs, or the hero clambering aboard from his horse and stopping a runaway wagon. The importance of the family unit as a central pillar of society is always reinforced in these films. In *West of the Divide* (Bradbury, 1933, Monogram/ Lone Star), the storyline is (as it is so often) about a single businessman attempting to use underhand methods to buy out local smallholders, but the key focus is on Ted Hayden (Wayne) reclaiming a family for himself. He has the task of avenging his father, who has been murdered but, in the process recreates a family unit, finding his younger brother (who sees him not only as his older brother but also very much as a father figure) and, of course, marrying the girl.

In *Riders of Destiny*, the Wayne character, Singin' Sandy, is fond of a threatening song that ends, 'Tonight you'll be drinking your drinks with the dead.' It is only ever the 'baddies' that have the piece directed at them, but it remains a rather dark lyric for a 'singing' hero. The recurring interest (as in A-Westerns from the period) is in strong central characters forced to take the law into their own hands. This trend is extended in some other films to the point where the 'good' characters become vigilantes. *Westward Ho* (Bradbury, 1935, Republic) has an opening title, 'to the Vigilantes.' Here, Wayne (as John Wyatt) puts together a vigilante group known as 'The Singing Riders' who, dressed in black outfits with white scarves and white horses, employ lines referring to 'the midnight dream of terror.' In *The Night Riders* (Sherman, 1939, Republic), 'Los Capaqueros' ('the hooded ones') clad in white hoods and cloaks evict Spanish landowners in California who have obtained their land through deception.[16]

The key Western from the late 1930s and part of a shift back to A-Westerns is John Ford's *Stagecoach* (1939, United Artists/Walter Wanger Productions), a film that seems to anticipate changes to the Western that will occur in the 1940s. Comparing it to *The Big Trail* from the start of the decade, this film pays its respects to the grandeur of the Western landscape but avoids attempting to be 'epic' in the conventional sense. Instead, it focuses on the human drama of intense personal and social relationships played out within a confined space. The contradictions of the genre are contained in its central character, the Ringo Kid, a strong individual seeking personal revenge but wanting to be a simple farmer. The 'baddie,' Luke Plummer (Tom Tyler), is killed by Ringo in a classic, if distinctively filmed, final shoot-out, but Ringo is himself an outlaw who has escaped from prison. 'The law' has not only jailed the wrong man but failed to offer justice and, as a consequence, it has been down to the strong individual to put things right. In a similar vein, *Jesse James* (as with a series of gangster movies from the '30s) also displays sympathy for 'outlaws' who have been wronged. Here, Jesse (Tyrone Power) and his brother, Frank, (Henry Fonda) are seen as fighting against the railroad to save their mother's farm. As in many other Westerns, the

Figure 2.2   James Stewart and Marlene Dietrich (*Destry Rides Again*, 1939)

incursion of powerful, moneyed interests is seen as a threat that leaves the individual with little choice but to fight back.

An altogether different attitude toward law and order is taken in *Destry Rides Again* (George Marshall, 1939, Universal). Thomas Jefferson Destry (James Stewart) believes absolutely in law and order but without the use of guns. The corruption in the town of Bottleneck focused around the Last Chance Saloon is made clear in the first 20 minutes of the film before Destry arrives as deputy. To the amazement of all, when he does arrive he is not wearing guns. For the next hour, Destry attempts to turn things around through persuasion and show that gunplay never really solves anything. Ultimately he fails, and the final minutes of the film turn into a full-scale battle between the forces of good and evil as Destry buckles on his guns and the men of the town turn out to back him in taking on the 'gangsters.' Clearly there are debates here about law and order, and corruption, that may be as relevant to what is happening in American cities at the time as any city-based crime film. However, in the year that war breaks out in Europe and as the United States debates whether it should become involved or not, there may be further obvious issues at stake. British prime minister, Neville Chamberlain, is following a policy of appeasement with Hitler. Politicians in

America are arguing that the United States should maintain an 'isolationist' foreign policy. Destry appeases the forces of evil but eventually has to strap on his gun belt. Incidentally, there is also a Russian character who, despite being a source of comedy, also becomes allied strongly to Destry. And, finally, complicating the entire issue, the women of the town intervene, minimizing the bloodshed by marching between the two sides before defeating the corrupt elements in their own way.

WESTERNS IN THE 1940s AND 1950s

The 1940s and 1950s are seen as the period of the classic Western. Yet, what is meant by 'classic' isn't easily defined. The most obvious feature of Westerns in these two decades is the sheer range of the films being produced: *Northwest Passage* (Vidor, 1940, MGM) is from the sub-genre of Westerns set in colonial America; *They Died With Their Boots On* (Walsh, 1941, Warner Brothers) offers a highly romanticized version of the West; *The Ox-Bow Incident* (William A. Wellman, 1943, 20th Century Fox) presents a dark, foreboding, noirish perspective on the West; *Duel in the Sun* (Vidor, 1946, Vanguard Films) pushes at the boundaries of sexual censorship; *Broken Arrow* (Delmer Daves, 1950, 20th Century Fox) is among the first revisionist Westerns; *The Naked Spur* (Anthony Mann, 1953) might be called a psychological Western; *The Tall T* (Budd Boetticher, 1957) is what many would think of as the 'classic Western,' a lone man setting out to exact revenge; and *Terror in a Texas Town* (Joseph H. Lewis, 1958) is a B-movie that demonstrates that low-budget Westerns continued to offer interesting perspectives on the genre during this period.

The classic era is often seen as being set in motion by John Ford's *Stagecoach* (1939) but not really getting underway until after the Second World War. *Stagecoach* combines thematic and stylistic elements of the popular B-Westerns from the 1930s with much more careful character investigation and a distinctive vision of the nature of the Frontier. Through the second half of the 1940s (*My Darling Clementine* [1946, 20th Century Fox]; *Fort Apache* [1948, RKO/Argosy]; *She Wore A Yellow Ribbon* [1949, RKO/Argosy];

Rio Grande [1950, Republic/Argosy]); and into the 1950s with *The Searchers* (1956, Warner Brothers/C.V. Whitney Pictures), Ford continued to explore the main themes of *Stagecoach*: prejudice, hypocrisy, and what he saw as the emergence of key moral standpoints and ideals during the period of the Old West. It is not an overall position that is easy to pigeon-hole, being in many ways reactionary but yet containing strong liberal elements. It is certainly, though, a distinctive, personal version of the mythical 'West.'[17]

In general terms, characters in Westerns after 1945 begin to have more doubts and uncertainties. They also begin to display darker aspects to their makeup even as they fulfill the role of the 'hero.' Good and bad, and justice and injustice, can no longer be seen in such comfortably black and white terms by the audience. Western filmmakers begin to offer a greater variety of ways of seeing (and, therefore, ways of understanding) the West. A confident vision of the grand sweep of American history as an inevitable, onward march of progress is lost. Central characters are no longer so likely to be the strong, silent individual who stands out as a leader of men but are darker, more troubled characters who are unsure of their role, place, and function in relation to the community. And, the uncertainty of these men is made palpable for the audience, who within many Westerns are increasingly likely to find their views being challenged. Westerns tend to move into towns and urban and domestic spaces, where light and shadow, props and costume, shot composition and angle, increasingly tell of fraught personal relationships and inner struggles. What seems to be happening is that Westerns are incorporating, knowingly or unwittingly, elements of the emerging genre of film noir. The darkness of the final scenes of *Stagecoach* takes over the whole of *The Ox-Bow Incident* (1950) and plays a critical role in further films, such as *Duel in the Sun* (1946); *Pursued* (Walsh, 1947, Warner Brothers); *Ramrod* (Andre De Toth, 1947, United Artists/Enterprise Productions); *Blood on the Moon* (Robert Wise, 1948, RKO); *Yellow Sky* (Wellman, 1948, 20th Century Fox); *Devil's Doorway* (Mann, 1950, MGM); *The Furies* (Mann, 1950, Paramount/Wallis-Hazen Inc.); and *High Noon* (Fred Zinnemann, 1952, United Artists/Stanley Kramer Productions). 'No longer a place of expanse and possibility, the Frontier began to appear as a dead end,' according to Drew Casper (2007: 342). In *Yellow Sky*, outlaws from a violent, male West find themselves in an increasingly dark ghost town inhabited only by 'Mike' (Anne Baxter) and her grandfather. In *Devil's Doorway*, a Civil War vet, Robert Taylor as 'Broken Lance' Poole, finds himself in a dark world of ongoing racial hatred. In *Return of the Bad Men* (Ray Enright, 1948, RKO), Randolph Scott (Vance) is the good-guy marshal who finds himself pitched into the midst of night-time gunfights, and Robert Ryan (Sundance) is a dark, sadistic killer.

Scott Simmon (2003: 230) suggests a group of postwar Westerns made in the few years immediately after the conflict show potentially strong characters who are confused about how they should take action. The opening to *My Darling Clementine* shows Wyatt Earp and Doc Holliday watching a performance of Hamlet's soliloquy, 'To be or not to be,' from Shakespeare's play, *Hamlet*, in which the lead character seems to debate how and when to take action. Simmon mentions *Along Came Jones* (Stuart Heisler, 1945, RKO/International Pictures/Cinema Artists), *Pursued* (Walsh, 1947, Warner Brothers), and *Angel and the Badman* (James Edward Grant, 1947, Republic/ Patnel Productions) as showing central characters in the same bind. He might have gone on to mention *High Noon*, made five years later, that sees Gary Cooper as a lonely, isolated individual struggling to come to terms with the need to take action in the knowledge that doing so might mean his death. In *The Gunfighter* (Henry King, 1950, 20th Century Fox), Jimmy Ringo (Gregory Peck) spends the film waiting and waiting for the final gunfight that will bring about his death. By contrast, in *Angel and the Badman*, Quirt Evans (John Wayne) is able to leave a past of guns and gunfighting behind. He is reformed, inevitably by the love of a woman but less expectedly by the love of a pacifist Quaker family, and defended by an honest and upright lawman, Wistful McClintock (Harry Carey), who concludes the film's debate with the line, 'Only a man who carries a gun ever needs one.'

There is also a new sensuality emerging in Westerns after the war. *The Outlaw* (Howard Hughes, 1943, United Artists/Hughes Productions) featured Jane Russell as Rio McDonald, whereas *Duel in the Sun* focused the camera on Jennifer Jones as Pearl Chavez and was quickly nicknamed 'Lust in the Dust' by the public. The second of these films will be considered more fully later, but *The Outlaw* also offers a clear example of a film attempting to push the boundaries of censorship in the period. Gregg Toland's cinematography

Figure 2.3   Jane Russell (*The Outlaw*, 1943)

adds some classy touches, employing lengthy tracking shots, point-of-view shots, and deep focus to good effect, but the plot outline is one of the film's most intriguing aspects. Jules Furthman uses a framework of two love triangles. The first is quite conventional being between 'Doc' Holliday (Walter Houston), Rio McDonald, and Billy the Kid (Jack Beutel), although the way it is employed is startlingly 'male' and underscores the masculine reaction to women frequently found in Westerns. Billy, for example, justifies his relationship with Rio to 'Doc' by referring to the fact that 'Doc' has been using his horse ('You borrowed from me: I borrowed from you'). Throughout the film, the fact that women are not to be trusted is emphasized and this is reinforced by the fact that the second love triangle is between three men: Doc, Billy, and the sheriff, Pat Garrett (Thomas Mitchell). The central driving emotional force for the storyline is the anger felt by Pat when Billy takes Doc away from him. The dislocating shifts in genre from drama to comedy and the accompanying sudden changes in Mitchell's character, from a comic fall-guy to being darkly psychologically driven, mean the film lacks overall coherence. However, the essentially B-Western coating that we end up with may have been one of the few ways of bringing material with clear homosexual overtones to the screen in the early 1940s. The more immediately obvious aspect of sexuality in both this film and *Duel in the Sun* is the display of the female body. The focus of the camera is often on aspects of Russell's body; one scene, for example, has her serving food to the three men at a table so that her head is cut off by the shot and her breasts 'float' along the top of the shot between the men. Again, however, it could be argued that the script pushes the boundaries even further. Billy returns at one point, for example (it seems with the intention of shooting Rio for having double-crossed him and Doc), and the script has him say, 'Will you keep your eyes open? Will you look right at me while I do it?' before we fade to black.[18]

With the Western being increasingly set in small emerging townships, there is now the opportunity within the genre to show a community taking shape. Interpretations of these approaches often see these 'communities' as standing for society at large. Key questions at the back of the films seem to revolve around what the nature of this new community (i.e., America) should be and, in particular, what values it should adopt. Often individual gunmen are shown as coming into the town and setting it on the path toward being an idealized 'community.' Those who are a threat to the new emerging township and its way of life are moved out by Earp in *My Darling Clementine*. The 'gorillas' as he calls them have been cleaned out of Black Rock by the time McCreedy (Spencer Tracy) leaves the town in *Bad Day at Black Rock* (John Sturges, 1955, MGM), and the community is explicitly said to have another chance to remake itself. Of course, within such a pattern sometimes the community might not measure up as in *High Noon*, Zinnemann's attack on the failure of society during McCarthyism. Additionally, all the time, these interpretations are finally the province of the audience. At the end of *My Darling Clementine*, Earp leaves town; he, too, it seems has no place in the new community, but other viewers of the film might (and have) seen it differently.

Ford's third cavalry film from the period, *Rio Grande*, offers a useful way of seeing Westerns from this period in relation to history. The film begins and ends with a shot of the 'Stars and Stripes,' so its patriotism is clearly stated. On a domestic level, the plot revolves around cavalry officer Colonel Kirby

York (John Wayne), who has been separated from his wife and son for 15 years. War (in the plot, the Civil War, but with a clear historical parallel in the Second World War) has brought about the breakup of a family, and now the wife and husband have to get to know each other again, and the father has to establish a relationship with his son for the first time. Eventually, the plot reunifies the family, re-establishes the family unit and, in the process, re-emphasizes the social importance of this institution. On a political level, the plot involves dealing with a war-like enemy, the Apaches. This group, which clearly threatens the previously mentioned family unit in that it attacks a wagon train of women and children, continually retreats across the border into Mexico where the Army has clear orders from the politicians not to go. Finally, a general gives Col. York the covert order to ignore this 'soft' approach being pedaled by the politicians:

> I want you to cross the Rio Grande, hit the Apache and burn them out. I'm tired of hit and run. I'm sick of diplomatic hide-and-seek.

The film takes a clear position: the United States has to be prepared to cross borders even to resort to clandestine operations (York's reply to the above line is, 'I've waited a long time for that order, sir, which of course I didn't hear') to deal with enemies to the American way of life. If we stop to consider what this means, we realize the film is suggesting that at times it is necessary to move beyond democracy, that it is necessary for the military to take decisive action that has not been approved by politicians or by the public.

WESTERNS IN THE 1960s AND 1970s

Out of necessity, the Western genre that came out of the United States was reshaped in the 1960s: the nature of the cinema audience in that country and around the world was changing, and films, if they were to be economically viable, had to reflect something of this alteration. Cinema was being challenged as the pre-eminent form of popular entertainment and not just by television; for young people, youth culture was evolving into a dynamic social force around the medium of rock music. This music was rebellious in its instrumentation, vocal sounds, and performance and crystallized the revolt of a sizable proportion of a generation in a form that through technology was able to find widespread expression. The currency of this 'new' dynamic music became magnified in its potency as a younger generation of Americans with a newly acquired voice began to be drafted halfway around the world to fight in Vietnam. The development of the Western in a sense paralleled this evolution of popular music. The genre had always had its darker ambiguities, but now there was no glossing over of these uncertainties; instead, they were directly addressed, brought to the forefront and highlighted to leave the audience challenged (maybe, in some senses, disturbed) rather than comforted. To make the point again: this should be recognized as, in fact, only a slight change of emphasis. Ethan Edwards (Wayne) in *The Searchers* from the mid-1950s, for example, is a dark, disturbing character and the hero who restores order.

Leonard Quart and Albert Auster (1984: 91) speaking about the war film, *The Green Berets* (1968, Batjac Productions/Warner Brothers), directed by and starring John Wayne, note that:

> No longer could Wayne's war-loving, patriarchal figure, spouting the old patriotic and macho certainties and clichés about decent, freedom-loving Americans and brutal, totalitarian Vietcong, capture and dominate the moral centre of the American imagination as it once had.

There is some truth in this in relation to this film and in respect of the Western genre,[19] but it is also true (and needs to be remembered) that Wayne remained a top-ten box office star throughout the 1960s (and that, despite his known political perspectives and as the example of *The Searchers* demonstrates, Wayne could be used within films in a more complex way).

In *Ride the High Country* (1962, MGM), Sam Peckinpah took up themes, in particular the passing of the old West and the difficulty of adapting to changing times, to which he would return in his most famous Western, *The Wild Bunch* (1969, Warner Brothers/Seven Arts Productions). The world within the historic moment of the film is changing, but so too is the contemporary world within which Westerns are being made. Characters have to adapt or die within the narratives, and Westerns are faced with the same choice. What doesn't change thematically, it seems, is the genre's fascination with the necessity for personal values, ideals by which to live. In *Ride the High Country*, Steve Judd (Joel McCrea) dies but not before he has ensured the redemption of his aging friend, Gil Westrum (Randolph Scott).

As mentioned earlier, this is the period of the Vietnam War, which was at its height in the late 1960s and early 1970s, and something of this experience is reflected in the Westerns of the time, not least in Peckinpah's *The Wild Bunch*. Some filmmakers clearly felt it was no longer possible to construct Westerns as narrative myths in which ritualistic violence was played out disconnected from any photographic revelation of the reality of death and mutilation. The violence being reflected on newsreels from Vietnam began to be reflected in Westerns. Media audiences for the first time were experiencing vivid visual first-hand accounts of frontline war in newsreels.[20] Controversy surrounded the war, with anti-war protests and demonstrations for peace taking place across America, particularly in universities, and yet, Peckinpah's film was not a box office success, and the graphic violence was seen by many as a disturbing trend.

In *The Wild Bunch*, there are no 'good guys,'[21] and this is a feature of films from the period. Clint Eastwood as the Man With No Name may be portrayed as ultra-cool in the opening to *Fistful of Dollars* (1964, Constantin Film/Jolly Film/Ocean Films, Italy-Spain-West Germany), for example, but he is a mercenary and a killer who earns money through using his gun, as do the gunfighters in the earlier film, *The Magnificent Seven* (John Sturges, 1960, Mirisch/Alpha Productions/United Artists). However, perhaps this amounts to the emergence of a new kind of hero for a new era, a hero who is more cynical, more worldly-wise, more self-seeking, but who in the end makes the same choice as of old in acting in defense of the weak over the strong.

Certainly, with the emergence of 'spaghetti' Westerns, notably those of Sergio Leone (*A Fistful of Dollars, For a Few Dollars More* (1965, Arturo Gonzalez Producciones/Constantin Film/Produzioni Europee Associati, Italy-Spain-West Germany) and *The Good, the Bad, and the Ugly* (1966, Arturo Gonzalez/

Figure 2.4 Graphic violence (*The Wild Bunch*, 1969)

Constantin/PEA, Italy-Spain-West Germany), the Western genre lurches abruptly into a new era of cinematography (and, interestingly, a new sound era, witness Elmer Bernstein's work on *The Magnificent Seven* and Ennio Morricone's work on Leone's films). Leone's distinctive visual style in which, for example, wide-screen landscape long shots are juxtaposed with extreme close-ups of eyes or hands and Peckinpah's highly choreographed scenes of extreme violence, move the Western into new areas. Their approaches further suggest that the old Western and the old Western hero can no longer be made to fit the times. This is made abundantly clear by Leone's use of Henry Fonda as a brutal villain in *Once Upon a Time in the West* (1968, San Marco/Rafran Cinematografica/Paramount, Italy-USA).

'Spaghetti' Westerns were filmed in Spain and Italy and, to some extent, emerged out of Westerns made in Germany in the early '60s that revealed a European market for the genre.[22] These Italian films often highlighted the corruption of the political and religious authorities and the difficulties faced by the poor in a society in which a small but powerful wealth-owning class took everything for itself. *Django* (Sergio Corbucci, 1966, BRC Produzione/Tecisa/Constantin Film, Italy/Spain) shows the genre being played with in new and extreme ways that invite the audience into a knowing, almost conspiratorial, relationship with the filmmakers. With production faltering in Hollywood (Radio-Keith-Orpheum (RKO) went out of business in 1957, Republic followed in 1958, and 20th Century Fox recorded losses through the early 1960s, for example), there were increased market possibilities for foreign films in the United States.[23]

To various degrees and using a variety of approaches, many homegrown American films from the period question the nature of both the 'Old West' and the Western genre. *Blazing Saddles* (Brooks, 1974, Crossbow/Warner Brothers); *The Outlaw Josey Wales* (Eastwood, 1976, Malpaso/Warner Brothers); and *Buffalo Bill and the Indians (or Sitting Bull's History Lesson)* (Altman, 1976, United Artists/Dino De Laurentiis/Lions Gate/Talent Associates) represent very different approaches to the Western, but each in its own distinctive way contributes toward revising America's view of its past and, therefore, of itself. In response to dynamic political interactions taking place nationally and internationally, cinema in the United States became more overtly political. The Western had always given the audience a particular perspective on the nature of America and to that extent had always been political, but now the willingness to take on political issues became both more conscious and more explicit.

The old Hollywood system of major studios controlling the production, distribution, and exhibition of films was finally broken in this period. Rather than directly employing all of the staff necessary to keep films rolling off a production line, one-off projects were put together, with teams of actors, filmmakers, and technicians signing up to make single films. The size of the cinema audience contracted, and the number of films being made dropped, but the search for a formula to attract audiences meant experimentation was possible. Marketing tactics such as having two-for-the-price-of-one star pairings heading up the film were tried and worked as with Paul Newman and Robert Redford in *Butch Cassidy and the Sundance Kid* (George Roy Hill, 1969, Campanile Productions/20th Century Fox). However, film styles also changed, reflecting in particular changes brought in by the French New Wave in the early 1960s and opening increased possibilities for directors to operate as auteurs. With older generations increasingly staying at home, the youth market became ever more important. To attract this segment of the audience within the context of a dynamic sociopolitical period and a vibrant cultural context of new musical and artistic expression, the content and the style of films (including Westerns) had to change. *Little Big Man* (Arthur Penn, 1970, Cinema Center Films/Stockbridge-Hiller Productions), for example, offers a reinterpretation of almost every aspect of the American West as portrayed in earlier Westerns and, in displaying the brutality of the U. S. Army against Native Americans, sets up challenging parallels to Vietnam. *Ulzana's Raid* (Robert Aldrich, 1972, Universal/De Haven Productions/Associates & Aldrich) offers no heroes or villains; each character is inescapably bound into a position of helplessly playing out the unfolding events. There is unavoidable inevitability about the outcome of the clash of cultures and understandings of the world.

The number of Westerns produced by Hollywood may have fallen off in this period, but actually the '60s and '70s offer a rich vein of innovation in the genre. This is driven by a new global perspective that is taken on the Western. Not only are other national cinemas, significantly in Italy but also elsewhere, taking the genre and shaping it in their own ways but American filmmakers emboldened by political contexts of the period begin to stand outside of an isolationist U.S. national consciousness and view the American West in a more detached, analytical manner. A film such as *Black God, White Devil* (Glauber Rocha, 1964, Copacabana Filmes/Luiz Augusto Mendes Cinematograficas) at the start of the Cinema Nova movement in Brazil confidently takes elements of the genre and utilizes them within new national, cultural, and political contexts. Such enhanced reflexivity is even to be found in a Wayne star-vehicle such as *The Shootist* (Don Siegel, 1976, Dino De Laurentiis). Ed Buscombe suggests Wayne plays 'the honourable gunfighter out of place in the largely cynical modernity of the days following the death of Queen Victoria' (1991: 299); but, more to the point, the old construct of 'Wayne' is given expression as being 'out of place in the largely cynical modernity' of the '60s and '70s.

THE DECLINE OF THE WESTERN

The decline in popularity of Westerns was brought into sharp focus by financial problems with Heaven's Gate (Michael Cimino, 1980, United Artists/Partisan Productions). Subsequently, this film has been critically acclaimed by some but, at the time of its release, it had gone well over budget and was a box office flop that ended losing $38 million. The film ruined United Artists, which merged with Metro-Goldwyn-Mayer the following year.

Cimino was one of a group of directors permitted considerable freedom by Hollywood in the late 1970s to try to maintain profitability in the face of declining audiences.[24] These directors were sometimes given the creative room to expand their visions to epic proportions.[25] Directors such as Sergio Leone and Sam Peckinpah had already been allowed by the studios to update the Classical Hollywood style in line with 'new wave' developments in cinematography, editing, and sound that had emerged from Europe and elsewhere in the 1960s. The aim of the studios was to reshape their product to connect mainstream American films with what was by now a predominantly young audience. Westerns had appealed to earlier generations at a time when cinema was the dominant medium for visual entertainment, but that audience was now into middle age and spending their time at home with television for entertainment. For young people, classic Westerns were in effect historical dramas increasingly unrelated to their everyday lives in terms of norms, values, and outlooks. The genre was one aspect of American 'cinema de papa,' to borrow a term used by French New Wave directors to describe French cinema before they came on the scene. And yet, in the same year Heaven's Gate was released, The Long Riders (Walter Hill, 1980, Huka Productions/United Artists) made a profit of more than $20 million. So, although it is true that the genre is in decline, with fewer Westerns being made, and although it is true that the profile of the cinema audience is changing, it may be that Heaven's Gate simply failed to give mainstream punters what they wanted. Certainly, Pale Rider (Eastwood, 1985, Malpaso/Warner Brothers) seemed to serve up what was wanted a few years later, as it made $60 million. This film offered a much simpler narrative with a clearly defined sense of good and evil and a tried and tested format of a stranger arriving in a town in need of a hero. *Silverado* (Lawrence Kasdan, 1985, Columbia Pictures/Delphi III Productions) proved that really very little was demanded of the Western if it was to prove moderately successful in box office terms. The violence may be more realistic than that found in Hollywood Westerns of the '40s and '50s in the superficial sense of being more graphic and bloody, but this is a very traditional Western in which the heroes, although they may receive the occasional bloody beating, are utterly immune to death and certain to win the day. Both *Pale Rider* (particularly in its acknowledgment of changed attitudes toward sex) and *Silverado* (particularly in its cozy, Hollywood liberal use of a black central character) recognize the need to address with some awareness an audience with new outlooks, but both remain intensely conventional in their use of the genre.

The 1980s was a period of conservatism, a period of backlash against the left-leaning political challenge of the '60s and '70s. President Ronald Reagan, a cowboy actor himself from the classic period,[26] came to power promising to restore 'the great, confident roar of American progress and growth and optimism.'[27] 'Reaganomics,' as his financial policies came to be known, involved tax cuts and business deregulation, confronting the unions and curtailing most areas of government expenditure apart from defense spending. To back up his foreign policy of 'peace through strength,'[28] he oversaw a buildup of arms to confront the Soviet Union, backed anti-Communist movements around the world, and ordered the invasion of Grenada and later the bombing of Libya. *Heaven's Gate* is born on the cusp of a political transformation in the United States, a swing to the right, and is out of keeping with the new mood.

Revisionist Westerns that take a more critical look at the way in which the historical period of the American Frontier has previously been represented figure more strongly in the 1990s. *Dances With Wolves* (Costner, 1990, Tig Productions/Majestic Films) offered a politically correct reappraisal of the representation of Native Americans, allowing the Lakota Sioux in particular not only a metaphorical voice for their culture but the literal use of their own language. *Unforgiven* (Eastwood, 1992, Malpaso Productions/Warner Brothers) offered a reassessment of the grim brutality of Frontier life, allied to an unflinching assessment of a complex central character who, although he was to some extent in line with the confident administrators of justice Eastwood had previously played, was made more disturbing for the audience by being played as a real human being rather than a genre fantasy figure. These two films presented a stronger challenge to the conventional Western in terms of storyline, characters, and themes than Westerns in the 1980s and achieved financial success into the bargain. Other films in the early 1990s, such as *The Ballad of Little Jo* (Greenwald, 1993, Joco/PolyGram) and *Posse* (Van Peebles, 1993, PolyGram/Working Title, UK-USA), although they did not achieve the status of being Oscar-winners like *Dances With Wolves* and *Unforgiven*, were in the same revisionist mold. *The Ballad of Little Jo* has a female central character who, to survive in a West populated by predatory males, dresses in traditional Western male attire and successfully passes as a man. The misogyny of the West is fully explored but not before the hypocrisy of upper-class Eastern families has also been highlighted by the way in which the central character, Josephine, who is to become Little Jo, is ostracized for bearing an illegitimate child. In a racial subplot, Little Jo saves a Chinese man from being lynched and crosses a further taboo boundary in becoming his lover. In *Posse*, the issue of race is brought to the fore in such a way as to expose not only the prejudice faced in the West in the nineteenth century but that of the Hollywood film industry that had largely excluded African Americans from the Western genre, effectively (and comfortingly, for large sections of the white audience) writing them out of Frontier history.[29] *The Quick and the Dead* (Sam Raimi, 1995, TriStar, USA-Japan) takes a more populist 'feminist' approach than that found in *The Ballad of Little Jo* by placing Sharon Stone in the lead role as a gunfighter avenging the death of her father.[30] In the process, she also operates in classic Western style as the stranger who enters town to save ordinary folk from the bullying attentions of an embodiment of evil (John Herod played by Gene Hackman). This film offers traditional sentiments from the Western genre (Russell Crowe's line, 'Killing people's wrong' receives the retort from Stone, 'Some people deserve to die') alongside a recurring conventional Western storyline but with a woman in the central role.

At the same time, there was a continued investment in more traditional Westerns such as Tombstone (Russell, 1993, Hollywood Pictures/Cinergi

Figure 2.5   Sharon Stone as a female gunfighter (*The Quick and the Dead*, 1995)

Pictures) and *Wyatt Earp* (Costner, 1994, Warner Brothers/Tig Productions/ Kasdan Pictures), both of which revolve yet again around reinterpretations of the Gunfight at the OK Corral in Tombstone in 1881 between the Earps and the Clantons. The radical differences between these two films highlight the way in which what the audience is witnessing with the Western genre is not in any sense the reality of the historical moment, or event, but an interpretation, or representation, of that history, a fantasy purporting to contain some 'truth' with relevance for the contemporary world. *Wyatt Earp* works hard to reinforce the old Western belief that 'Outside of family, the law's about the only thing to believe in' (Gene Hackman as Nicholas Earp, Wyatt's father). Further, the father also aims to inculcate his sons with the belief that there are 'evil men in the world' and that when you meet one 'you have to hit first and hit to kill.' However, this attitude could be seen to be questioned as the older, increasingly cynical Wyatt becomes colder and effectively a familial tyrant. This means the film barely manages to contain an uncomfortable central ambiguity. The postscript ending showing Wyatt Earp as an older man goes some way toward re-establishing his iconic image, but never fully outweighs the impact of the earlier vision of a character reduced by life to a brutal, vengeful man.[31]

In the last decade, *Brokeback Mountain* (Ang Lee, 2005, Alberta Film/Focus Features/Good Machine/Paramount/River Road) has shown the Western continuing to be used to explore aspects of American history in a revisionist style and displayed the genre's refusal to be contained within a classic late-nineteenth-century framework. *The Assassination of Jesse James by the Coward, Robert Ford* (Andrew Dominik, 2007, Warner Brothers/Jesse Films/Scott Free Productions/Plan B/Alberta Film/Virtual Studios) has shown the seeming requirement of the Western to continually work and rework legends of the period in the currency of the present day and displayed once again its refusal to be contained within the classic space of the land west of the Mississippi.[32] Two years earlier, *The Proposition* (John Hillcoat, 2005, U.K. Film Council/Surefire Films/Autonomous/Jackie O Productions, Australia-U.K.) had taken the Western into the interior of an entirely different continent. *Open Range* (Kevin Costner, 2003, Touchstone Pictures/Cobalt Media/Beacon Pictures/Tig Productions), given the subtitle or tag line of 'No place to run, no reason to hide,' conversely, shows a return to the key location, period, and interests of the Western. Here, we are in Montana in 1882 witnessing the struggle between the cowboy way of life involving driving cattle hundreds of miles across open range to railheads and a more settled style of farming involving the fencing off of tracts of land with barbed wire. The name of the film announces a belief in a key aspect of American self-consciousness, namely that the United States is an open country where people are free to 'range,' or roam. The image is one of freedom, and it embodies a set of related, maybe mythical (but no less powerful for that) beliefs about America. The subtitle tells the viewer exactly how this film suggests America should feel about itself in relation to international terrorism. Two years after the 9/11 attacks and in the year of the invasion of Iraq by American and British forces, this is the Western announcing once again that there are evil men in the world that have to be confronted and that at that point what society has to have is a gunfighter who is a good man but is capable of killing ruthlessly if necessary.

CONCLUSION

The vast generalizations that emerge with any historical survey of a genre point toward the ultimate impossibility of fitting the range of films being produced into any overarching vision. The so-called classic period of the

Western during the 1940s and 1950s, for example, clearly saw a multitude of contesting perspectives on the Western presented to audiences. There are trends that can be identified. Historical events such as the Depression of the 1930s and the Vietnam War did have an identifiable impact on Westerns being produced. And yet, the historical approach remains no more than suggestive, a useful starting point for your own investigation of the films.

To consider one additional context: filmmakers unavoidably operate within the wider media. They work within one strand of the mass media, a mass media that through the historic period of filmmaking have had an increasingly intimate relationship with and influence upon society. Films and filmmakers, like all other media and media professionals, mediate between events in the real world and an audience or, if you like, society. They reshape events that in some form have taken place in the real world – pioneer families did cross the American interior in wagon trains, wars were fought with the Native American indigenous populations, lawless new towns did develop across the West, a railroad was built that did cross the continent, cowboys did (briefly) drive cattle herds to railheads to be transported east – into a narrative to be consumed by an audience. This is a process of interpretation involving the selection of elements for inclusion and others for exclusion, the imagining of contexts only partially documented, and the centring of certain characters and marginalization of others. This interpretation takes place in accordance with professional training and within the constraints of the medium. It also reflects the ideological perceptions of the filmmakers and exists in relation to the socio-historical moment of production. The resulting films may not only have a range of possible effects on individual spectators but may, in various ways, influence the nature of society.

As an audience, much of what we know and believe about the world is arrived at in this second-hand way through the mediation of films or television, or books or newspapers. Our way of seeing the American West, which amounts to a particular fluid, evolving, dynamic way of understanding a particular version, or representation, of the world, is shaped by the way these events are presented to us. This process could be seen as a channeling of consensual social knowledge and cultural values, but it should also be acknowledged that the representations of the American West we receive are arriving through the interventions of filmmakers operating from particular ideological standpoints. The reading of genre films can become no more than a routine so that audiences begin to take for granted the deep ideological assumptions embedded in these films.

Investigating how the interface between the Western film text and its audience might be seen to function and how the relationship between these films and the wider society might be seen to operate requires the application of a range of theoretical approaches. This is what will be attempted in the next chapter of this book.

NOTES

1. The extent to which we can describe these films as 'Westerns' is debatable as the term comes into frequent use only after about 1920.
2. See Marianne Bell's *Frontier Family Life: A Photographic Chronicle of the Old West*, p. 109, for a photograph of the interior of Colorado's Cripple Creek Saloon.
3. In the 1830s, five Indian tribes were forced to march from the South to newly designated Indian Territory west of the Mississippi. Thousands died along the way.
4. The poses taken up here echo Frederic Remington's painting *The Last of His Race* (1908). In his paintings, Remington generally foregrounds his human characters and offers the landscape as little more than a washed-out backdrop. Of course, the choice can still be made as to which characters to foreground and in which ways. In *Last of His Race*, for example, Remington foregrounds his Indian in a sympathetic manner, as 'noble' rather than 'savage.'
5. This narrative device might be said to continue to operate in some form in future Westerns. For example, in *Dances With Wolves* (Kevin Costner, 1990), a white woman is able cross the divide and then return to bring some sense of a closer understanding between the races.
6. The opening titles of this film proclaim it 'A tale of the sturdy Americans whose life-work was the conquest of the Great West.'
7. Lieutenant Colonel George Armstrong Custer's detachment of more than 200 men from the 7th Cavalry are wiped out at the Battle of the Little Bighorn in 1876. Accounts of the battle vary but the legend of 'Custer's Last Stand' quickly developed.
8. The confidence displayed by politicians and writers in both periods was immense. 'America is such a garden of plenty, such a magazine of power, that at her shores all the common rules of political economy utterly fail,' wrote Ralph Waldo Emerson in 1883 (Emerson, 1903: 105).

9. 'If a race is weak, if it is lacking in the physical and moral traits which go to the make-up of a conquering people, it cannot succeed' (Roosevelt, 1896: 2).

10. A set-piece with the same title was the popular climactic feature of Cody's Wild West Show from 1887 onward.

11. 'Experienced wranglers and cowboys came to work in the movies, and actual outlaws and lawmen acted as 'technical advisors.' Outlaw Emmett Dalton, for example, moved to Los Angeles in the twenties and even wrote movie scenarios, while both Wyatt Earp and Pinkerton agent Charles Siringo were photographed watching the action on movie sets (Hughes, 2008: xi).

12. Detailed accounts of the wagon-train treks to Oregon and California during the 1840s are given in Frank McLynn's *Wagons West: The Epic Story of America's Overland Trails*.

13. In Ford's *Stagecoach*, made in the same year, the banker Gatewood is just as corrupt, again attempting to make off with the bank's money.

14. Wayne's voice was dubbed, but the full 'singing cowboy' films that emerged particularly in the second half of the decade and throughout the 1940s (most famously starring Gene Autry, Roy Rogers, and Tex Ritter) effectively became a musical-Western hybrid.

15. 'Parched farmers could not pay mortgages, and banks foreclosed on their property. Suicides and divorces soared.' (Tindall and Shi, 2007: 1039)

16. A second version of the Ku Klux Klan emerged in 1915 and lasted until 1944. In the five years following the First World War 'the entire West, especially the southern plains, experienced an eruption of KKK activity' (Etulain and Malone, 2007: 81). This group now saw Catholics and Jews as much as African Americans as the 'un-American' enemy.

17. 'Living in his imagined nineteenth-century Eden ... the director created his own recognizably "Fordian" value system, a reflection of his own inner desires and conflicts.' (McBride, 2004: 420)

18. See Darwin Porter's *Howard Hughes: Hell's Angel* for the behind-the-scenes story of this film in relation to censorship of the time.

19. In fact, *The Green Berets* is a Western only loosely disguised as a war film: for Vietcong read Indians, and for cavalry read American Special Forces. As with the nineteenth-century Indian Wars, there are no front lines, for example, and so, like Indians in Westerns, the Vietcong are shown as being capable of appearing out of nowhere to attack.

20. This type of media coverage of war was, perhaps, with the Vietnam conflict available for the first and only time. Subsequently, it might be argued, material reaching viewers has been much more carefully managed by government departments.

21. Disturbingly, the gang led by Pike Bishop (William Holden), are dressed as soldiers when taking part in the opening 'blood-bath' scene in town.

22. During the period, Hollywood is also looking to tailor its products more carefully to the European market. Around half of U.S. box office income was coming from abroad by the mid-1960s, up from just a third before the war. (Thompson and Bordwell, 2002: 328)

23. 'Between 1969 and 1972, the major film companies lost $500 million.' (Thompson and Bordwell, 2002: 513)
24. Steven Spielberg (*Jaws*, 1975) and George Lucas (*StarWars*, 1977) had created the 'blockbuster,' a must-see social event, designed to attract audiences back to the cinema.
25. Cimino's earlier Vietnam film, *The Deer Hunter* (1978), was 3 hours long, and Francis Ford Coppola's *Apocalypse Now* (1979) lasted 150 minutes.
26. Playing George Armstrong Custer in *Santa Fe Trail* (Michael Curtiz, 1940) and a hired gun in *Cattle Queen of Montana* (Allan Dwan, 1954), for instance.
27. http://www.whitehouse.gov/about/presidents/ronaldreagan
28. American Security Council Foundation. Strategy Board, Coalition for Peace Through Strength (1984) *A Strategy for Peace Through Strength*. Ann Arbor: University of Michigan.
29. Or, as with John Ford's use of Pompey in *The Man Who Shot Liberty Valance* (1962, Paramount/John Ford Productions), placing the African American in the classic position of loyal servant. It might be observed that, in this case, it is Pompey who is pointedly shown in the classroom reciting from the *Declaration of Independence* that 'all men are created equal,' but it would be difficult to deny that this is handled in a patronizing fashion.
30. Whether simply placing a woman in the role of the hero could be seen as a genuine feminist approach to the genre is, of course, highly debatable. Perhaps there would be similarities to the debate around Sigourney Weaver's being cast as Ripley, the gun-toting hero in *Alien* (Ridley Scott, 1979). See Annette Kuhn's *Alien Zone: Cultural Theory and Contemporary Science Fiction*: 'Ripley, indeed, is hardly female … she is confused with her male companions and denied any sexual difference at all' (1990: 106).
31. Happily, the film does at least confirm some improvement in Costner's acting abilities from nine years earlier in *Silverado*.
32. *The Last of the Mohicans* (Michael Mann, 1992, Morgan Creek Productions/20th Century Fox) had in the previous decade taken the Western back as far as the late 1750s and the struggle between England and France for control of the American colonies.

3

THEORETICAL AND CRITICAL APPROACHES TO WESTERNS

WESTERNS AND GENRE

Focus films: *Gunfight at the OK Corral* (John Sturges, 1957, Paramount) and *Bad Day at Black Rock* (Sturges, 1955, MGM).

At this point, we will return to the concept of genre discussed in the Introduction and attempt to apply aspects of genre theory to two films directed by John Sturges. One aspect of genre theory is the suggestion that each film type has its own iconography: characteristic props, costumes and settings, for example, that act as visual signifiers alerting the audience to the genre of the film they are watching.[1] This visual context is very obvious in *Gunfight at the OK Corral* wherein the men ride horses, wear classic Western-film-style cowboy boots and hats, and carry handguns. Just a couple of minutes into the film as three strangers enter the saloon, the camera focuses in ominous close-up on the gun and holster on the hip of one of the men. Guns and 'gun-play,' it is clear, are set to dominate the action. However, the concept of iconography also refers to the use of sound signifiers and visual signifiers; these might be musical signifiers (characteristic features of the soundtrack) or verbal signifiers (characteristic features of the dialogue).[2] Within minutes of the opening of *Bad Day at Black Rock*, Lee Marvin's character, stretched on a bed so that his cowboy boots and hat are forcefully presented, is given the line: 'I believe a man's nothing unless he stands up for what's rightfully his: what do you think?' This is classic 'Western-speak.' The underpinning issue of 'manhood' and what is to be understood by this may be undermined by the line's being given to a bully and by Spencer Tracy's character, John Macreedy, replying with a very understated, noncommittal, 'I guess so,' but if we are familiar with the Western genre, we immediately understand what is at stake and what will be effectively under discussion for the duration of the film. Later, the town's 'Doc,' talking to the sheriff, takes up the theme: 'There comes a time, Tim, when a man has just got to do something.' And so, allied to the visual signifiers and sound signifiers, further signification of genre is at work. Themes such as what constitutes the 'just' and 'unjust' use of force or violence or the nature of masculinity are constantly re-examined.[3] Similar character types and character relationships, such as the threatening bully and the emotionally controlled hero, are also worked and reworked.

A music signifier operates as a key component in the opening to *Gunfight at the OK Corral*. It announces even within the first few seconds before any characters emerge that this will be a Western. How does a simple orchestral sound achieve this? There is no arrangement of musical notes that is inevitably and obviously linked to Westerns simply as a result of some inherent property of the notes as arranged. As with visual images, the sounds we are presented with can signify only as a result of an experience of past Westerns

Figure 3.1   Lee Marvin (*Bad Day at Black Rock*, 1955)

shared by both the producers of the film and the audience. In essence, if genre communication is achieved, it is because a shared language exists that makes signification possible. We learn the language of any genre through experiencing its use over time, so that, the more 'reading' we do within any given genre, the more fluent we become in its 'language.' Knowledge of the iconography of Westerns, along with an awareness of typical storylines, character types, and character relationships found in previous Westerns, contributes to the creation of audience expectations of what they will be most likely to see in the rest of the film.

In everyday use, 'genre' is a simple term we all understand, so much so that this understanding can appear almost instinctive. Those for whom the Western is not a genre they usually spend time watching will still often recognize the type of film they are dealing with from the opening bars of the film soundtrack of *Gunfight at the OK Corral* and certainly from the first few visual images. The screen is split in two, divided between an expansive yellow prairie and a vast sky, and the scene is given the sound backdrop of a whistled tune accompanied by a clip-clopping sound effect reminiscent of horses' hooves. Three dark outlines of figures on horseback come over a ridge, emerging out of a sea of grass, and ride slowly toward the camera. Every element of this opening comes from the back-catalogue of the genre. When one of them bends from his horse to lift a post and remove a section of fence blocking their route, he throws it carelessly to the ground. It is a simple action, but it is entirely appropriate and is echoed shortly afterward when, as they enter a saloon, the first of the three men violently pushes open the door. However, notice how we have moved beyond a genre analysis to deal with performance: ways of opening doors or casting things to the ground would be found in all sorts of films. Signification is at work, but it is not specifically genre signification. The implicit suggestion throughout this section of this book will be that genre operates as one form of analysis but takes its place among others and is effectively used only in harness with other forms of approach to film.

The opening lyrics of the song heard at the start of *Gunfight at the OK Corral* with the repetition of 'OK Corral, OK Corral' will locate the film very clearly within a particular Western legend (an infamous shoot-out in 1881 in Tombstone, Arizona; see Andreychuk, 1997: 61–72; Barra, 2009; Blake, 2006; Luhr, 1996: 23–44) for enthusiasts of the genre, but this will place this group only marginally ahead of other viewers in their understanding because these words come only shortly before the film's title blazes its way across the screen with the key opening genre word of 'gunfight.' The fence (probably barbed wire, thereby reinforcing the positioning of the film as post-1873) we see stretching across the prairie, a seemingly innocuous prop unless you are familiar with the genre, symbolizes a key Western opposition between homesteaders and cattle barons for those in the know. However, if they failed to respond to this image, the mass audience will find themselves sure of their genre just a moment later when the three riders enter the classic Western one-street town with wooden buildings, verandas and boardwalks.

The opening to the second film, *Bad Day at Black Rock*, is in many ways entirely different, and yet there are more than enough signifiers for those with the requisite genre knowledge to categorize this as a Western. The color palate, although in this case corresponding to a landscape that is more desert than prairie, is again dominated by yellow but here tending towards 'hotter' orange hues. A train slices through the landscape at speed placing the film in the twentieth century (and perhaps suggesting danger and a sense of urgency), but the train will also be seen by those who are familiar with the genre as a further key icon of the Western.[4] In this film, rather than opening by focusing on three dark shapes that by their actions when they enter the foreground straightaway denote themselves as 'baddies,' we see our central character almost immediately. However, in both films, the audience is immediately taken into an isolated, one-street town where everyone turns to look when a stranger, or strangers, enters. The first person our central character, Macreedy, meets on stepping from the train is a telegraph operator linked by his job to a technology credited like the train with 'opening up' the West to civilization. In classic Western style, we have a lone man entering a town he is destined to 'clean up' before leaving at the end having enabled the town to move forward into the future as a morally redeemed community. In keeping with this familiar narrative strand of Westerns, Macreedy is immediately referred to as a 'stranger.' As with Wyatt Earp (Burt

Lancaster) in Gunfight at the OK Corral, he is the strong, quiet-spoken outsider who is relied upon by the community to restore order by taking into his own hands the administration of justice. When we first see Earp, he is the lone rider coming into town, shot from a low camera angle to emphasize his importance to the narrative and his stature among the story's characters.

However, among all of these characteristics of the genre, the most interesting element of any genre film is the way in which it counterpoints the norm. The audience desires to see their expectations fulfilled, but they also receive additional pleasure from finding those same genre-created expectations undercut or challenged in some way. The most obvious feature of Bad Day at Black Rock to achieve this is the setting of the recognizable Western story in post–Second World War America. In Gunfight at the OK Corral, among the classic scenes of confrontations in saloons, cattle-drive cowboys hitting town, and male camaraderie on the open range, as we move toward the denouement, we are suddenly and unexpectedly confronted by dark noir-like scenes. Earp becomes a dark 'hero' driven by revenge, a character of the shadows moving as if weighed down by doubt in Lancaster's performance. Sturges very deliberately begins to juxtapose shots of women as the long-suffering voices of reason against the violence of the male code of honor.[5] The presence of the director who is common to both films adds a further complication. The image of hunting might be one that is common to Westerns, but could it also be seen as part of the director's 'signature' placed on the film and therefore an element more relevant to an auteur approach than a genre approach?[6] In Bad Day at Black Rock, Reno arrives with a dead deer tied across the front of his car; there is a deer's head trophy on the wall of the sheriff's office and in the hotel; and in Gunfight at the OK Corral, deer's head trophies or bison horns decorate the walls in a series of scenes. Furthermore, mirrors are used in both films with an interesting further use of reflections in the hotel windows in Bad Day at Black Rock. This would seem to owe more to the director's personal approach than the genre of the film. However, what should we say about the presence of lynch mobs in both narratives? This is a genre feature, but also, it might be argued, a particular element of Sturges's approach. In the face of the unleashing of this pack-like activity (to spell it out, a hunting activity), all 'Doc' Holliday can do in Gunfight at the OK Corral

Figure 3.2   Wyatt Earp (Burt Lancaster), a character of the shadows (*Gunfight at the OK Corral*, 1957)

is get out of town, whereas in *Bad Day at Black Rock*, the aftermath of what is effectively lynch law forms the basis of the whole narrative.[7]

Both films feature the expected final shoot-out in which the 'baddie' is defeated and order restored to the community. Here we begin to overlap with narrative analysis because, of course, this is an outline of the resolution phase of a classic narrative structure. In a sense, neither is a conventional Western showdown. In *Bad Day at Black Rock*, Macreedy is unarmed and resorts to an entirely unconventional 'weapon,' a hurriedly improvised petrol bomb. In *Gunfight at the OK Corral*, although most Western enthusiasts will already know the outcome of one of the legendary Old West gunfights, they may not know enough of the historical detail to be expecting the final part of the shoot-out to take place in a photographer's shop. The input of the director (or the collective unit working on the film) again seems important. The imagery of a camera, family photographs, (rather bizarrely perhaps) birdcages, and the youngest of the Clantons retreating upstairs into the photographic darkroom before being shot adds considerably to the potential meanings available to the audience.[8]

So, these two films exhibit general similarities to a succession of other movies in the same genre and, yet, ultimately each is distinctive in the ways in which it uses or adapts ideas common to its genre. Each of these films employs scenarios that recur throughout the history of the genre, but within this common approach each uses the available possibilities in its own way.

At the end, Earp's anguished 'Don't make me do it' as he tries not to have to shoot a younger brother, who reminds him (and us) of his own younger brother, adds depth to the story and characterization; but it also potentially shifts the ground toward a theme of concern throughout Hollywood films of the 1950s, 'troubled youth,' and what to do with it. However, we are again wandering beyond what might strictly be called genre analysis.[9]

WESTERNS AND SEMIOTIC ANALYSIS

Focus films: *Forty Guns* (Sam Fuller, 1957, 20th Century Fox/Globe Enterprises) and *Once Upon a Time in the West* (Sergio Leone, 1968, San Marco/Rafran Cinematografica/Paramount).

Semiotics[10] provides the basis for all other forms of analysis and has been implicit in the previous consideration of genre. Our apparently 'instinctive' understanding of a genre, in fact, is built on an acquired knowledge of the 'language' of a genre. A series of visual images and an array of sounds carry meaning only if we know the relevant genre language; every element of *mise en scène*, cinematography, editing, and sound operates within sign systems, or codes, to communicate meaning to the viewer. Body movements, for example (whether within a film genre or within everyday life), make sense only within a culturally agreed sign system of body language. The success (or failure) of such attempted communication depends on the extent to which a shared knowledge of the code, or sign system, exists between the producer(s) of the attempted communication and the audience. Individual shots, scenes, and sequences in films are constructed, or put together, out of 'signs' that are being used to communicate with the audience. Close-reading enables us to 'unpack' the film text, exploring potential meanings and associations.

As the historical era in which Westerns have tended to be set was closing and as films dealing with this period were beginning to create the genre of the Western, the philosopher, C. S. Peirce (d. 1914), suggested there were three types of sign: an 'icon' resembled the object described – a photograph, for example, indicated something beyond itself by direct resemblance to that object; an 'index' worked through a direct link between sign and object – smoke, for example, indicated something beyond itself (i.e., fire); a 'symbol' had neither direct resemblance nor direct connection to the object indicated but only an agreed cultural link – in some cultures a red rose, for example, has a culturally agreed link to the idea of love.[11] Film is clearly dependent upon 'icons' at a fundamental level, but indexical signs and symbolic signs are also at work within screen images. 'Six-guns' in Westerns, for example, operate indexically, being directly linked to bullets and shooting; and a train, or simply a railroad, has a symbolic link within the genre to the concept of 'progress' as both a threat to a past way of life but also the promise of the future development of America.

Developing these ideas in the 1970s, Roland Barthes suggested a sign had a simple, surface or literal meaning at the level of 'denotation' and a further potential set of meanings at the level of 'connotation' consisting of the social and cultural associations linked to the sign.[12] The mechanical process of photography (or cinematography) produced denotative meanings, displaying simply the surface fact of, for example, 'This is a woman,' or 'This is a man.' However, the image maker's intervention – use of camera angle, distance, focus, shot composition, cropping, editing, props, costume, lighting, and the like – produced connotative meanings. Within the second level of meanings, 'myth' was also at work, where 'myth' was an interlocking set of concepts widely accepted within a culture as expressing their understanding of some aspect of social experience. So, portraying Native Americans in Westerns as primitive, for example, might reinforce a shared dominant social belief in American society

Others (Fiske and Hartley, 1978) suggested connotations and myths attaching to visual images expressed a further level of signification, or meaning, that of ideology. Stuart Hall (1973) suggested that in decoding images, a reader might adopt the socially dominant, preferred meaning or construct a negotiated reading, accepting some parts of the preferred meaning but rejecting others, or adopt an oppositional reading, totally rejecting the preferred reading.[13] Overall, what is emphasized by semiotics is the importance of basing any critical analysis on close attention to the

Figure 3.3   Barbara Stanwyck as powerful woman (*Forty Guns*, 1957)

nature of individual signs and the relationship of these signs to concepts conjured up in the reader's mind. The final meaning of any sign might be closely dependent upon the social context within which the audience experiences it. If, for example, the country is in the middle of a war, an on-screen battle takes on a particular resonance, as does the presence of a threatening 'outsider' figure.

The two films under discussion here are in many ways very different, but both have an underpinning concern with an anticipated impending end to the Old West. In *Forty Guns*, the central female character, Jessica Drummond (Barbara Stanwyck), tells the central male character, Griff Bonnell (Barry Sullivan): 'This is the last stop, Griff: the Frontier's finished.'[14] In *Once upon a Time in the West*, both Frank (Henry Fonda) and 'Harmonica' (Charles Bronson) know the coming of the railroad spells the end of their gunfighting way of life. Both films have openings that make their genre immediately clear, both incorporate early shoot-outs displaying dramatic action after periods of uneasy calm, and both use final climactic shoot-outs that have been continuously postponed while feeling increasingly inevitable throughout the film. They are both, therefore, clearly marked out as Westerns.[15]

In the opening to *Forty Guns*, a man drives a flat-back open wagon along a dusty road with two male passengers sitting behind him. They hear the thunder of hooves before a woman on a white horse going in the opposite direction gallops past them at the head of 40 other riders to a soundtrack of dramatic music. The signs at work here are largely iconic in Peirce's terms in that we are presented with a series of images directly resembling implied objects. So, for instance, the photographic images of horses stand for implied objects in the real world. In Barthes's terms, men, horses, a buckboard, and a woman are simply denoted. However, in semiotic terms, signs are also at work in other ways in this sequence. The sound of horses' hooves would be, in Peirce's terms, indexical; a direct connection to the implied objects (horses) is exploited to create a mental concept for the viewer attaching to those sounds without the viewer actually seeing any horses. The blond hair of the female character is simply iconic — it is just there in the image as blond hair but could also be seen as symbolic, implying a culturally agreed connection to female beauty and, maybe in filmic terms, to dangerously alluring female beauty. Certainly, in Barthes' terms, the black clothing this woman wears has a series of potential connotations attaching to it — black is especially associated with bad, or evil, characters in classic Western imagery. She is also wearing trousers, which are simply at one level denoted (or shown) as trousers but, again, there are several potential connotations, especially when linked to the fact that the woman's clothing (both trousers and shirt) seems to be tight-fitting.[16]

In the opening to *Once Upon a Time in the West*, three men arrive at an isolated railroad station and settle down to await the arrival of the next train. Guns are a key sign from this early sequence in the film, with particular focus being placed on a handgun when one character uses the barrel of his weapon to trap a fly that has been annoying him. The gun — a sign with connotations of death and violence — is used in a light comic fashion that only serves to enhance the ominous threat of the denoted object that is dwelt upon in a series of close-ups. In a similar way, a series of images simply display people, places, and objects associated with a railroad — a stationmaster, rail tracks, and heavy rail timbers — indexically suggesting the concept of a train. However, beyond this, the implied train in association with the visually present railroad is also symbolic, having culturally agreed associations with technological progress, the 'opening up' of the West, and the bringing of civilization to previously barbaric regions. In Barthes' terms, these connotations present the idea of 'train' as a cultural myth, a sign that embodies dominant values and ideas. In this reading of the signs, trains are associated in a positive way with relentless, onward human progress, provided you share certain cultural values.[17] The water tower and the name on the side of this structure — 'Cattle Corner' — are both further interesting examples of signs. Clearly we have a photographed water tower, and therefore, in Peirce's terms, an iconic sign resembling the implied object. However, the sign of the water tower implies the concept of 'water' by direct associative linkage and so also operates as an indexical sign. Furthermore, the same image of a water tower operates on a symbolic level implying the vital importance of water to survival and to 'progress' in such an arid region. In Barthes' terms, the simply denoted water tower carries with it the same sorts of connotations as might be seen as symbolic associations or meanings in Peirce's terms. In association with other signs so far seen, in particular the range of guns, the water tower would also carry the connotation of water's being such a vital resource in such a place that in both historical reality and other Westerns it has been the source of bloody conflicts.

The opening shoot-out in *Once Upon a Time in the West* is a classic fully fledged gunfight. However, in *Forty Guns*, although it is set up as a classic scenario with the hero walking along the main street toward the young man who is the source of trouble in the town, the audience is denied the gunplay while still being left in no doubt about the hero's courage. Griff uses the handle of his pistol to club Brockie Drummond, thereby avoiding killing him. Again, the sign of the handgun is strongly presented, indexically alerting the viewer to the directly connected objects of bullets and thereby maybe to ideas of shooting and killing. Certainly, from Barthes' perspective, these sorts of connotations would be present; the gun as sign carries with it an entire hinterland of associative potential meanings. These potential meanings may be activated at this stage in the narrative or at some later stage, or they may be undercut by what happens. In this case, with the audience anticipating gun play as a result of the series of signs with which we are presented – two men with guns facing each other on a dusty Wild West street – the actual outcome is different, and we are reminded of a further potential meaning attaching to the gun as sign, that these objects can (as we have seen in the past) be used as clubs.[18] The young man being essentially disciplined by the older man may (now, as we look back at a film from the 1950s, or potentially at the time as well) remind the audience of a further associative meaning 'built into' the sign 'young man': in general terms, It has often been seen that 'young men' need to be disciplined by the older generation and, in specific terms, it is often suggested that 1950s American films frequently address the issue of 'young man' as rebel. Peirce was interested in the way in which signs needed to be seen in sociological and linguistic terms, and this was the entire thrust of Barthes' work. And, here we are really beginning to address this linkage: the underpinning of sign usage by actual social realities. To explore this any further, we would need to consider not just the sign system accompanying the presentation of Brockie but also in particular that which works to give us an understanding of the role and status of Chico, Griff's seemingly happily subservient younger brother. These two characters offer directly opposed positions for the younger generation to adopt.

Before leaving this initial 'shoot-out' in *Forty Guns*, it is worth considering one further link between these two films: the way in which both directors use close-ups of the face. As Griff walks down the street, Fuller employs a series of close-ups of his eyes.[19] In terms of signs, it is clear that much more is at work here than a simple iconic representation of eyes. However, here, rather than social connotations, the associations at work might seem to have much more to do with suggestions about character. The eyes, shot in this way with this performance and this intensity of cinematic gaze, work as a sign to indicate indexically (or should that be symbolically) a certain type of character – a strong, determined hero. However, notice that if this is the interpretation that accompanies this sign as presented, it does have clear social implications in that it does reflect a dominant belief system that elevates such a hero to a position of key narrative importance. Through his use of close-ups, Leone places even greater emphasis on facial expressions in *Once Upon a Time in the West*. Seeing each of these shots as a sign intimately linked to a series of other signs and, therefore, part of a sign system operating within the film would provide part of our starting point for an analysis of these facial expressions. However, again, it would be important also to see each of these shots in relation to wider social systems of signification.

The final shoot-out in *Once Upon a Time in the West* offers an enhanced classic scenario in which the protagonists, rather than walking toward each other, seem to circle each other in ballet-like opening movements to their dance of death. Frank's death is the death of the old way of life

Figure 3.4   Sergio Leone's use of close-ups (*Once Upon a Time in the West*, 1968)

in the West, replaced by the coming of civilization symbolized by the rail tracks' being relentlessly and unstoppably laid in the background. The mouth-organ, or harmonica, is the most powerful single sign at work in this final sequence. Its significance in relation to events preceding the start of the film has been made clear through a series of flashbacks, but its use most powerfully enables a sound to be given to the final breathe of a dying man.[20] The sign is not simply a denoted object but an image with layers of potential meanings. The shoot-out at the end of *Forty Guns* also employs a twist on the classic confrontation by having the 'baddie' use his sister as a human shield only for the 'hero' to calculatedly shoot her first before mercilessly killing his opponent. 'Woman' is denoted by the photographic image of Stanwyck as Drummond, but the connotations attaching to the concept of 'woman' within dominant value systems seem to be brutally undercut by the hero's cold response. In fact, the strength of the male in the 'male–female' relationship is being reinforced as is the implied social need for men to forcefully control women.

Any understanding of these two films must start from engagement with individual signs as used by the filmmakers. When Wes is fitted for a new gun by the gunsmith's daughter in *Forty Guns*, we understand the sexual foreplay at work only if we read images as not simply denoting objects but as carrying connotations. When Frank sits behind Moreton's desk in *Once Upon a Time in the West* and discusses the nature of power, the desk is clearly more than just a desk. When we move to compare scenes such as, perhaps, the funerals found in both films, we need to compare, for example, the different connotations attaching to the very different coffins used. Each is simply a prop operating as a sign denoting a box for a body, but each carries different connotations. The roughly hewed coffin in *Once Upon a Time in the West*, for example, suggests poverty, hardship, and the harsh nature of life in the West. In *Forty Guns*, 'God has his arms around me: I'm not alone' seem to be words from a set-piece song that is presented without irony in a way that would be unimaginable in *Once Upon a Time in the West*.

WESTERNS AND REPRESENTATION

Focus films: *They Died With Their Boots On* (Raoul Walsh, 1941, Warner Brothers); *Run of the Arrow* (Sam Fuller, 1957, Globe Enterprises/RKO); and *Dances With Wolves* (Kevin Costner, 1990, Tig Productions/Majestic Films).

The issue of representation is central to analytical approaches to film as it considers the way in which reality is being depicted and the resulting meanings generated for the audience. It is useful to think of 'representation' as 're-presentation,' as this carries the suggestion of a process of construction. Commonly, representations are considered as reflections or distortions of reality. Representation is often seen as the attribution of certain characteristics to individuals or groups, but places or events will also be re-presented to the viewer in certain chosen ways. These representations (often amounting to culturally accepted stereotypes) might be seen as either 'negative' or 'positive' in their ramifications or, to pick up a word from semiotics, connotations. Richard Dyer (1985) suggests the key issue is to explore texts in terms of who is representing whom and in what ways. Which voices are dominant? Who is silenced? Who is at the centre of the text? Who is marginalized? This type of analysis will lead to the identification of issues of power and the revelation of the workings of ideologies within the texts. It would be possible to consider the representation of an entire range of areas of social classification such as race, national identity, regional identity, class, gender, and sexuality in Westerns, but primary focus here will be on the representation of Native Americans.

> How we are seen determines in part how we are treated; how we treat others is based on how we see them; such seeing comes from representation.
>
> (Dyer, 2002: 1)

The view of George Armstrong Custer given in *They Died With Their Boots On* may be both immeasurably generous to the historic figure and inflated in both heroic and romantic terms (Niemi, 2006: 27–28), but the treatment of the 'Indians' is in several ways progressive for the period. For any filmmaker tackling this subject, there is no escaping the fact that the single fact for which Custer is best known, the Battle of the Little Big Horn, was an Indian victory. Inevitably, any viewer will be waiting to see how the final known element of the biography is represented. And, in the final battle scenes, Custer's tactical inadequacies are fully displayed; the only thing he knows about cavalry strategy, as he admits from the outset of the film,[21] is to locate the enemy and charge. In doing so, he immediately falls into the trap laid by the Sioux. However, in the weeks immediately

Figure 3.5   Custer as romantic hero (*They Died With Their Boots On*, 1941)

after the historical event, in line with his celebrity status, newspapers and magazines presented Custer's Last Stand as a defeat, but a glorious defeat, and therefore, in a sense a victory. And this film takes the same approach. The 'defeat' is a victory for the central tenets of Custer's life and the final imperatives of the film – honor, integrity, and glory. When the 'entrepreneur' Sharpe asks before the battle where the regiment is riding, Custer's reply is: 'To hell, Sharpe, or to glory: it depends on one's point of view.' In this film, it is not the Indians who are presented as evil but the rampant greed of capitalists such as Sharpe.[22] Indians are certainly a threatening presence, often being represented through the cinematography as the unseen observers waiting to attack when cavalry or settlers are at their most vulnerable, but they are also to be admired as when Custer praises Crazy Horse's escape as involving brilliant horsemanship. When they are represented in a more conventionally mainstream style – 'A few thousand savages have stopped the march of American civilization' – we find the words are those of Sharpe's father, another capitalist businessman. If the film's use of inter-titles is seen as giving a clue as to the film's attitude toward the history of the period, the filmmakers would seem to see the demise of the Native American way of life on the plains as inevitable in the face of 'progress':

> And so was born the immortal 7th US Cavalry which cleared the Plains for a ruthlessly advancing civilization that spelled doom to the red race.

However, it is Custer's wife, Libby, after his death, who pronounces the film's final word on the Indian question:

> The Administration must make good its promise to Chief Crazy Horse. The Indians must be protected in their right to an existence in their own country.

Historically, Native American tribes were continually seen as politically expendable, but the filmmakers are suggesting an idea more relevant to 1942 than 1876. The phrase 'in their own country' in the foregoing quote reiterates a point made earlier by the very public-school Englishman in

Custer's 7th Cavalry, Butler, when the question of whether, as someone who is not really an American, he should go into the final battle is discussed.

> Not an American: what do you Yankees think you are? The only real Americans in this merry parish are on the other side of the hill with feathers in their hair.

Native Americans gained a reputation for their willingness to join the American forces during World War Two.

> One story made the rounds in early 1942 about a band of Apaches who collected their weapons and went to their Agency Superintendent to tell him they were ready for war. 'Why do Apaches need training to make war?' they asked him incredulously.

> (Nash, 1985: 130)

The representation of Indians in this film may employ Anthony Quinn rather than a native American as the main Indian character, it may give this character a stereotypical broken command of English ('You give word not kill with rope.'), and it may be underpinned by implicit essentially racist attitudes ('the red race'), but it repeatedly recognizes the rights of 'Indians' as Americans and acknowledges the less than honorable way they have been treated in the past.[23] In fact, of course, alongside the racist labeling of Native Americans as 'savage' and without civilization, there had been a patronizing representation of the Indian as a 'noble savage' throughout cinema history (and before this in literature). In places, indeed, recognition of their alternative, even in some senses superior, civilized values had found voice.[24]

These themes of the honor and civilization of the Native American are continued in both Run of the Arrow and Dances With Wolves. However, these later films go much further in this direction in that the distance (the pre-Civil Rights Movement segregation) between Indians and white Americans, which is maintained in They Died With Their Boots On, is closed by having central characters who 'go native.' The representation of Native Americans undergoes marked changes. Essentially, segregation is maintained in They Died With Their Boots On but begins to be questioned by the time of Fuller's Run of the Arrow. Custer (as a character in They Died With Their Boots On) may believe in honoring treaties, but his only response to issues of race is separation. When he arrives at Fort Lincoln, his first command is: 'I want every Indian put outside this fort.' And here there is a link to the earlier part of the film wherein the marginalized 'outsider' is African American rather than Native American. Blacks are present at Custer's wedding, but Walsh shows them as clearly segregated not only within the imagined space of the story but within his shot selection. Hattie McDaniel's performative presence as Callie in this first half of the film far outstrips the work of both Errol Flynn and Olivia de Havilland, but this is down to the vivacity of her acting. She dominates every scene in which she is placed despite the effort of the form to utilize her as nothing more than comic relief, and in doing so she exposes the way in which the script and cinematography attempt to marginalize her as a black woman. Quinn might be given more apparent status as the leader of a critical grouping within the narrative, but he is only permitted to present himself as 'the noble Indian chief' and is, unlike McDaniel, unable to take the material he is given and move beyond its limitations.[25] All of which points to the way in which the treatment of Native Americans in each of these films might also be seen to explore wider issues of racial difference within American society. The threatening background presence of Indians in each of these films (think of Crazy Wolf in Run of the Arrow and the Pawnee raiding party in Dances With Wolves) is potentially the threatening presence (from a white perspective) of all racial outsiders within American society. Perhaps, in this context, the casting choice that often seems to be made in Westerns to employ Hispanics or Latinos as 'Indian' characters deserves to be further explored. Of the three films, only Dances With Wolves employs Native Americans to play Indian roles; for example, Graham Greene (Kicking Bird) was ethnically from the Oneida tribe, Rodney A. Grant (Wind in His Hair) from the Omaha tribe, and Floyd 'Red Crow' Westerman (Ten Bears) was a Sisseton-Wahpeton Lakota Sioux. More immediately noticeable is the use of the Lakota (Sioux) language in this film. When young children were taken from Indian reservations and placed in special colleges during the late 1800s and early 1900s, a key emphasis was on stripping them of their own language.[26] This film restores the language and, in doing so, accentuates the

Figure 3.6   The Pawnee raiding party (*Dances With Wolves*, 1990)

use of the Native American point of view that begins to be explored in *Run of the Arrow*. The representation of Native Americans has moved from being that of a distanced 'Other' to an intimate presence with which both Dunbar and the viewer begin to identify. This identification is further consolidated with the intrusion of the brutal ignorance of the U. S. Army.

Run of the Arrow and Dances With Wolves strongly take up a theme of Westerns most famously displayed in the work of director John Ford: the beauty of the landscape. Both films show not only the awe-inspiring vast of expanse of the West but the idyllic lifestyle led by the Indian tribes. The campsite by the river filmed in *Run of the Arrow* is taken a stage further in *Dances With Wolves*, wherein each season is portrayed as having its own magnificent beauty. In both films, this landscape is clearly associated with the Indians and with their way of life:

> I had never known a people so eager to laugh, so devoted to family, so dedicated to each other; and the only word that came to mind was 'harmony.'
>
> (Lt. John Dunbar, Kevin Costner, *Dances With Wolves*)

Both *Run of the Arrow* and *Dances With Wolves* also demonstrate the potential brutality of 'Indians.' In *Dances With Wolves*, the blood-lust of an inter-tribal warrior culture is forcefully demonstrated, although we might note that when describing the zealous leader of the war party, one rather despairing Pawnee is given the line, 'He will not quit until we are all dead.' This is a theme from *Run of the Arrow* where Crazy Wolf takes pleasure in tormenting the old Sioux, Walking Coyote, before killing him and later operates as a renegade in breaking the agreement with the Army. In general in both films, the main Indian tribe, the Sioux, is seen as having individual chiefs who employ thoughtful reasoning and a strong collective sense of the importance of reasoned discussion.

Custer, the hero of *They Died With Their Boots On*, is directly referenced in *Run of the Arrow* as an example of the worst type of officer to be posted to the Indian frontier region:

> Col. Taylor: Here we are breaking our backs trying to make peace with the Indians and they send us officers like that scratching for combat.
>
> Capt. Clark: I guess he's not the only frustrated Custer in the Army.[27]

This is the heart of 'the Indian question' as explored in both *Run of the Arrow* and *Dances With Wolves*: the suggestion that ignorant, glory-hunting, Custer-like (and, in *Dances With Wolves*, 'uncivilized') Army types meant that white American accommodation with Native Americans was always in jeopardy. And this is why these two films are ultimately less interesting than *They Died With Their Boots On*. Both the later films develop the representation of Native Americans, creating something that is, in this respect, more accurate, but each of these films loses any sense of the rolling juggernaut of capitalism, 'a ruthlessly advancing civilization,' that is such a critical part of the representation of the West in the first film.

WESTERNS AND IDEOLOGY

Focus films: *High Noon* (Fred Zinnemann, 1952, United Artists/ Stanley Kramer Productions) and *The Alamo* (John Wayne, 1960, Alamo Company/Batjac Productions).

An ideological approach to film is based on the theory that all films put forward a particular view of the world, a way of seeing society and social relations. In this process, it is suggested, films implicitly (and often explicitly) promote a particular system of ideas and values, or set of beliefs; that is, they favor a particular ideology. Some critics have suggested ideology in Hollywood films operates as a means of controlling radical dissent:

> Rather than conceive of ideology as a simple exercise in domination, we suggest that it be conceived of as a response to forces which, if they were not pacified, would tear the social system asunder from inside.
>
> (Ryan and Kellner, 1990: 14)

But, some filmmakers might see themselves as actively offering a challenge to dominant social attitudes. *High Noon* was seen by screenwriter Carl Foreman as a condemnation of a society that allowed the McCarthyite political witch-hunt to take place in postwar America.[28] This interpretation of the film casts Senator Joseph McCarthy and others involved with the House Un-American Activities Committee as the Miller gang in *High Noon*, in other words as the 'baddies.' Furthermore, it suggests those who found themselves on 'trial' were, like Will Kane (Gary Cooper), effectively thrown to the wolves by a society unworthy of the name of 'community.'[29] By contrast, in *The Alamo*, John Wayne, as both director and star, sets out to give a heroic context to an episode in American history, which by implication modern America is expected to remember and live up to.[30]

Both of these films put forward a specific view of society; they carry a particular ideological perspective on the world. Interestingly, *High Noon* was read by many within contemporary American society as a condemnation of those who refused to back the Korean War. That is to say, the ideology contained within the film was seen to be something completely different from that identified by Foreman. Therefore, the ideology that is seen to be contained within any particular film would seem to depend on audience interpretation. What remains true is that each interpretation so far discussed recognizes that films have some immediate relationship to contemporary society and to how life should be lived.

An ideological approach sees films as being based upon a set of beliefs or understandings of the world. When the judge in *High Noon* decides to leave

Figure 3.7 The flag is taken down (*High Noon*, 1952)

town before Frank Miller arrives on the midday train to avenge himself, he takes down the U. S. flag and the 'scales of justice,' symbols of the essential values of American society. When at the end of the film Kane has virtually on his own defeated the Miller gang, he symbolically throws his sheriff's badge into the dust of the main street. The filmmakers present us with a society wherein the professed values are meaningless. Not only that, but the hero is allowed to show that he is scared of the task facing him.

> The movie set a precedent in Western films by showing a hero who is in no way superhuman, but who is instead quite capable of feeling fear while he is executing his duty.
>
> (Phillips, 1999: 117)

By contrast, in *The Alamo*, Wayne shows heroic men upholding without fear what they believe to be right, even to death.

In the same way his characters never show any doubt, so Wayne has his film set out from the beginning a position of absolute clarity and certainty.[31] The opening titles assert the 'tyrannical' nature of 'Generalissimo' Santa Anna's rule in Mexico in the mid-1830s. There is, therefore, according to the ideology (or belief system) of the film, a simple decision for settlers in Texas to make: '… the decision that all men in all times must face … the eternal choice of men … to endure oppression or to resist' (*The Alamo* – opening titles). The emphasis on the word *men* highlights the fundamental nature of the ideology found here. In short, it is founded upon the complete social dominance of (white) men. Women in this film are heavily marginalized. They are either sexually-aware dancing saloon girls, damsels in distress to be gallantly defended, or mothers and wives standing for the concept of family. The category of 'men' denoted in these opening titles is further complicated by the fact that it does not seem to include black men. Slavery was an important feature of the economy of Texas in the early 1800s.[32] The only African Americans in the film are a young boy and an old man; the young boy is used as a symbolic figure of innocence and shown to be fully integrated into a white family almost as if he a second child, and the old man is symbolically given his freedom just before the final assault on the Alamo but fulfills the stereotype of 'faithful slave' by choosing to stay and die with his white master, Jim Bowie (Richard Widmark). Within the framework of ideas constructed in the film, the old slave has to be freed, because Wayne as Crockett has defined the concept of the republic that they are trying to create in Texas as being a place where 'people can live free, talk free, go or come, buy or sell, be drunk or sober, however they choose.'

What belief system, or ideology, underpins *High Noon*, and how does it compare to that found in *The Alamo*? Justice is clearly seen as important,

Figure 3.8   The 'faithful slave' (*The Alamo*, 1960)

but the man who administers it, the judge, simply wants to get out of town when things get difficult. The flag would seem to symbolize certain rights, those rights given to citizens by the American Constitution, but in the face of opposition to all that it stands for, when it is most important for it to be flying, it is taken down. If we follow an interpretation that sees this film as responding to the McCarthyite political witch hunt of left-wing sympathizers, the suggestion would be that justice and the rights of individuals are being trampled upon in contemporary America of the 1950s. However, what does *High Noon* finally suggest, symbolized by Kane throwing his badge in the dust? Is it that society is not worth fighting for, that all you can do is defend yourself and escape (if you are lucky) to a quiet life with a young wife?

Both *High Noon* and *The Alamo* place a high premium on the concept of 'Right.' The narrative of *High Noon* depends upon our recognizing that Kane is on the side of 'Right,' fighting against that which is 'Wrong,' or 'Evil.' It recognizes that being on the side of 'Right' does not mean you automatically win: Kane's wife, Amy, says, 'My father and my brother were killed by guns. They were on the right side but it didn't help them when the shooting started.' Wayne's key speech in *The Alamo*[33] is:

> There's right and there's wrong: you gotta do one or the other. You do the one and you're living: you do the other and you may be walking around but you're dead as a beaver-hat.

This sentiment is at the heart of both films. This would be Zinnemann and Foreman's condemnation of those who turn away from justice and the rights of the individual.

The difficulty with the underpinning ideology in both films is the assumption that we all automatically, or naturally, know right from wrong and that we all agree what is right and what is wrong. Without acknowledging the extent of the problem for the film's basic ideology, *The Alamo* actually identifies the difficulty in its script. In a strong visual sequence displaying the brutal reality of war, after an assault on the Alamo, Mexican wives and mothers are shown searching among the dead for their husbands and sons, but the power of the scene is destroyed by the dialogue that follows as two Texan defenders try to make sense of what they have been involved in:

Sure killed many a brave man today.

Funny, I was proud of them; even when I was killing 'em I was proud of 'em. Speaks well for men that so many ain't afraid to die if they think right's on their side.

Ultimately, both films display a belief in a single strong man who is able to stand up to the forces of evil. Crockett dies in a final defiant gesture, blowing up the arsenal but, of course, through what he symbolizes and through the society that subsequently emerges in Texas and the United States, according to the ideology of the film, he lives on. Kane, in keeping with the genre formula but at odds with the realism of the first 70 minutes of the film, defeats the Miller gang and leaves town with the girl.

An ideological approach to film analysis suggests a society, such as America in the 1950s, will have a dominant set of 'norms,' or shared expectations of behavior, but the approach also recognizes that various social groups within a society will have their own 'norms.' Wayne's right-wing political beliefs, which reflect the dominant ideology in 1950s America, is clearly expressed in The Alamo. The central belief is in a particularly male form of martial heroism. However, when a viewer comes to the film, she may accept or reject the ideological outlook to be found there. Essentially, the viewer is free to agree, or disagree, with the 'messages' to be found in the film and so, unsurprisingly, particularly in a period of changing social values, 'the public response to Wayne's film was an odd mixture of acceptance and rejection' (Slotkin, 1998: 531).[34]

In the 1970s, cultural theorist Stuart Hall developed with others[35] an 'encoding/decoding' model for the transmission of messages in any form of mass communication. This incorporated semiotic analysis with theories of ideology and representation to study audience response to the media. As in semiotic analysis, the media message is understood as a complex series of signs, and both the production of media texts and their consumption are seen as social processes during which meaning (neither fixed nor inevitable) is constructed. During the encoding process, that is, the making of the film, ideological factors determine how the world is to be represented, or signified. Those involved in the process are not necessarily consciously aware of how their outlook and the outlooks of social groups to which they belong may be shaping the media text,[36] but that is what happens, so that the encoding process leads to the creation of a text that carries certain meanings.

However, the meanings ultimately taken away by the audience cannot be controlled by the encoders because the viewers will be decoding from their own ideological perspectives. The theory is that although a text may be heavily structured to push readers toward one interpretation, even powerfully constructed propaganda is always open to being rejected by its intended audience. In Hall's terms, the text will carry a preferred meaning[37] but, in decoding the film, viewers can make up their own minds how to see things. Hall suggested there were three possible viewing positions: the audience might take away the preferred meaning, or they might adopt a negotiated reading (taking on board some of the preferred meaning but not accepting the entire package), or they might construct their own oppositional reading, understanding the preferred meaning but rejecting it.

WESTERNS AND DISCOURSE ANALYSIS

Focus films: *Fort Apache* (John Ford, 1948, RKO/Argosy Pictures) and *She Wore Yellow Ribbon* (Ford, 1949, RKO/Argosy).

Following the work of Michel Foucault,[38] the term *discourse* has been understood to mean the shared ways of thinking, acting, talking, and representing the world found within a society. The suggestion is that in all forms of communication, shared patterns in the use of signs can be found. These shared patterns are discourses. Defined social groups are seen as having their own ways of thinking about particular aspects of society. These ways of thinking are then reflected in the way they talk and act and in the way they represent the world to others. And, as cinema is a form of representation, we should, therefore, be able to identify various discourses being employed

Figure 3.9   Nathan Brittles (John Wayne) beneath the 'Stars and Stripes' (*She Wore a Yellow Ribbon*, 1949)

within films. For example, one discourse found within both of the focus films used here is a discourse of patriotism verging on nationalism. The flag of the United States is continually employed as a symbol of values that it is assumed will be shared by members of the audience. A short way into *Fort Apache*, there is a scene in which we watch the 'Stars and Stripes' being ceremonially raised in the fort. The scene adds nothing to the narrative but has been placed very deliberately within the film. Why? What message are we supposed to receive? What discourse is being employed? Similarly, when Captain Nathan Brittles (John Wayne) receives his pocket watch from the regiment in *She Wore a Yellow Ribbon*, the composition of the shot we are given places him very deliberately beneath the 'Stars and Stripes.'[39]

Discourses are recognized as being able to shape people's attitudes, beliefs, and behaviors; essentially, to be able to influence their ideological perception of the world. Both of these films aim not only to put forward a series of representations of the importance of the American nation uniting beneath the 'Stars and Stripes' but to influence members of the audience to view the world from a patriotic perspective (or, if we are not citizens of the United States, presumably to acknowledge the stature of that country). The argument is that discourses do not simply reflect social reality in a neutral way but actively work to create a very particular understanding of the world. *She Wore* a *Yellow Ribbon* is deliberately set just after the defeat of Custer at the Battle of the Little Bighorn in 1876.[40] The scale of the defeat and resulting military pressure being placed on the United States armed forces is emphasized and personalized as Brittles slowly and deliberately reads the start of a list of the American dead (that is, white/U. S. Cavalry dead – notice how a discourse can appropriate a word such as *American* and give it a particular meaning), acknowledging that he knew many of these men. In historical reality, it was the various tribes of Plains Indians that were under most pressure, an intense pressure from the continual westward expansion of the white population. This is acknowledged in various more-subtle ways later in the film, but the opening effectively reverses the historical reality; it is the U. S. Cavalry (the embodiment of American values, and as such standing for the United States as a whole) that is presented as under threat. A voice-over tells the audience that 'From the Canadian border to the Rio Bravo 10,000 Indians … are uniting in a common war against the U.S. Cavalry.' A discourse is used that paints the Native American tribes as aggressors. They are 'on the warpath' while the cavalry is under threat 'wherever the flag rises over some lonely army-post.' Notice here the use of the word *lonely* filling the phrase with a sense of isolation and imminent danger. The particular Native American group given prominence in the narrative is Cheyenne Dog-Soldiers whereby the moniker used again sets up a sense of violent threat. Similarly, the way in which the opening image of a lone bugler in *Fort Apache* dissolves into a shot of mounted Apaches with prominent rifles moving right to left across the screen against the natural left-right flow for reading; the way in which the following shots of the cavalry are cut into by further shots of the Apaches with accompanying dramatic music; and the way in which the scene of a dance in the homely, civilized interior space within the fort where women are introduced for the first time is punctuated by a cut back to the armed Indians set up a discourse identifying Native Americans as a threat that lurks outside. The 'languages' of film, particularly editing, *mise en scène*, and music, have been used to structure a distinctive discourse.

Discourses, then, are culturally and socially produced sets of ideas and values contained in texts and representations. They amount to the articulation of abstract ideological versions of the world. And within a text, in our case

Figure 3.10 A lone bugler (Fort Apache, 1948)

within Western films, it is the prevalence of some discourses over others that establishes dominant, permitted ways of talking about (and therefore understanding) particular areas of social life. Discourse analysis is the investigation of these articulations of ideologies. It amounts to a synthesis of semiotics and ideology. Texts are analyzed as sign systems to discover meaning, and then, the relationship between those meaning systems and sociopolitical structures is considered. The effort is to identify the culturally and socially produced sets of ideas and values, that is, discourses, that are structuring the text and representations within that text. These latent or underlying systems of meanings within texts, it is suggested, both reflect and carry values. It is the job of discourse analysis to uncover or articulate these, in effect, abstract ideological versions of the world to be found within texts (and representations) that might normally go unrecognized.

The approach offered by discourse analysis enables us to see films as ideological structured. However, the overall discourse existing within any text is usually complex rather than simple: one strand of discourse may dominate, but others may coexist (perhaps uncomfortably) alongside it and within the same text. As has already been suggested, an alternative discourse on Native Americans exists within both Fort Apache and She Wore a Yellow Ribbon. This sees the Plains Indians as the victims of corrupt white men. In both films, traders licenced to sell goods to the Indians are represented as the real source of any problems there might be between Native Americans and white men. In both films, the character played by Wayne is able to speak with

Indians in an atmosphere of mutual respect and understanding. In the face of the abuse of his people by white profiteers, Wayne tells us in Fort Apache:

> Cochise did the only thing a decent man could do: he left, took most of his people and crossed the Rio Bravo into Mexico, rather than stay here and see his nation wiped out.

In She Wore a Yellow Ribbon, the troop commanded by Brittles comes across a herd of buffalo. This offers a visual spectacle but contributes nothing to the film's narrative. The scene is included as a reminder for the viewer of the way in which the way of life of the Plains Indians has been destroyed.[41] Again, the implication is that Native Americans should be seen as victims, not aggressors. This discourse of Native American as victim runs alongside the previously identified discourse of Native American as threat.[42]

A series of further discourses can be identified in both films. There is certainly a discourse on gender that identifies a clear series of roles for men and women. Men are to show gallantry toward women and display courage in battle (see Wayne in everything he does in both films centring this discourse as the key male role model). The main role of women is to support their men and uphold the importance of the home. They are homemakers (see, in particular, Mary O'Rourke [Irene Rich] in Fort Apache)[43] and mother-figures (see, for example, Abby Allshard [Mildred Natwick] with the two children orphaned after an Indian attack on their homestead in She Wore a Yellow Ribbon).[44] In a related discourse on romantic love, women in their younger years (Shirley Temple as Philadelphia Thursday in Fort Apache and Joanne Dru as Olivia Dandridge in She Wore a Yellow Ribbon) are expected to present themselves as flirtatious and controlling. However, ultimately both have to learn that they have been naively innocent about the brutal nature of the world about them. The recurring image of women found in both films shows them watching the men leaving for war and then awaiting their return. Relating this discourse to those so far identified with Native Americans, it is the absence of this focus upon Indian women and Indian community existence that is most noticeable. It could be suggested the absence of a discourse is as powerful in the determination of overall meaning within film as the presence of a discourse. Discourse analysis is particularly interested in the way in which power could be said to be embedded within a text. It is interested in the contest between particular points of view and emphasizes the way in which a film addresses the audience in a particular way that may exclude an entire series of further potential perspectives. What actually happened in American history regarding the Plains Indians or in the structuring of a woman's place within white communities in the American West is one thing: how these things are told or expressed within a particular discourse is another. Discourse analysis explores the connotations to be found in embedded preferred readings. Key questions for this approach are: how is the world represented in this text, how does this text see 'reality,' how does this text present 'truth,' what has been included and what has been excluded, and what has been marginalized and what has been emphasized?

Film hides its 'constructedness.' It presents itself as a straightforward representation (or mirroring) of social reality. In effect, it is hiding its operation as a discourse, a discourse with a particular ideological base. *Fort Apache* and *She Wore a Yellow Ribbon* present themselves as offering simple, direct perspectives on the world. In fact, both are highly constructed, expressing very particular discourses (and therefore ideologies). In any representation of any aspect of the social world, what is included and excluded is determined by the discourse at work (and this discourse is structured by ideology). Another way of approaching these two films using discourse analysis would be to group the discourses so far identified, under two headings: 'racist discourse' and 'patriarchal discourse.'

WESTERNS AND NARRATIVE STRUCTURE

Focus films: *The Big Trail* (Raoul Walsh, 1930, Fox) and *The Outlaw Josey Wales* (Clint Eastwood, 1976, Malpaso/Warner Brothers).

All narratives re-present the world to us in some form. It could be said that they recreate the world and give it to the viewer (reader, or listener) as some type of virtual experience or, that they interpret the world and give the viewer (reader, or listener) a version of that world. This telling of stories, the continual representation of the world in a multitude of reconfigurations, seems to be fundamental to human society. We seem to use narrative to make sense of, and to create meaning out of, otherwise chaotic experiences. In telling stories, order and shape are given to a series of events. From this perspective, narratives can be seen as particular arrangements of events within a structure. The 'plot' is the rearranged, highly selected chain of events given to the audience. At its simplest, this structure may be the relating of events in chronological order, but it can be more complex, with the reader being taken backward and forward through time. Flashback is used, for example, to tell the viewer how the hero found an old man who had been murdered in *The Big Trail* and, at points in *The Outlaw Josey Wales*, when the hero remembers a key moment from his past. Each element within the narrative will have cause(s) and effect(s). We come to any narrative expecting events that occur to be motivated in some way: to have been caused by something we have seen or heard earlier, and to have some discernible outcome, or effect.[45] Without this form of structuring, there would be only a random series of unconnected incidents. So, by definition, a story is an ordered series of events that leads to a conclusion.[46]

What structures are employed by Westerns? And, in what ways could these structures be seen as fundamentally the same as those that are used in other genres? Theorists have suggested all stories are structurally the same: we are introduced to a hero-heroine and shown the world in which they live, the normality of this world is disrupted, often by the appearance of some embodiment of evil, and the hero-heroine sets out to restore order. In basic terms, we deal with a scenario of heroes versus villains, or good versus evil, and a world in which order is set against chaos, so that all stories are founded upon the idea of a conflict between two or more central characters or groups of characters. However, the use of other techniques that complicate this, such as parallel episodes that form a deliberate contrast to each other, repetitions of events seen from different perspectives, and the integration of symbolic events or images to create significance, will also need to be considered.

In *The Big Trail*, Breck Coleman (John Wayne) is clearly presented as the hero of the piece. It is he who is followed by the camera at every significant

Figure 3.11   The cross gives way (*The Outlaw Josey Wales*, 1976)

point in the story. His mission is to find the killers of 'Old Ben,' be sure of their identity, and take revenge or, in his terms, administer 'frontier justice.' The villains are clear from the outset, their rough, uncouth attitudes contrasted with the clear-cut honesty of the hero. In *The Outlaw Josey Wales*, the hero is again central to everything that happens. His mission is to find the leader of the marauding Northern band of 'Redlegs' who killed his wife and son during the Civil War and to take revenge. Both films could, therefore, be categorized simply as 'revenge Westerns,' although, at least initially, there would seem to be significant differences. 'Old Ben' is a friend of Coleman's, but Josey Wales (Clint Eastwood) is linked much more closely to the victims. The opening, exposition phase of the narrative in *The Outlaw Josey Wales* uses all the devices of film construction to show the effect on the hero of his close-knit family unit's being brutally torn apart. As he buries his son, for example, the cross that he leans on in such a way as to make it into a crutch symbolically gives way beneath him. The audience is, therefore, prepared for the merciless way Eastwood as Wales dispatches a series of 'baddies' who cross his path. Wayne as Coleman seems to have a much colder, more detached perspective on the entire thing:

> Those two men killed a man in cold blood and they've got to pay. Not that I've got hatred in my heart, but I'm the law out here that's all, and the law is justice.

Both films see their hero as dispensing some form of 'justice' that doesn't depend on what might more usually be recognized as law and order but on a vigilante approach, or what Coleman calls 'frontier justice.'

Both films use the opening, or exposition phase, of the narrative to set up certain expectations for the audience. Key characters, ideas, and possibilities for the development of the story are introduced. The Big Trail makes clear from the outset the importance for the film of the concept of pioneering families' opening up the American interior as we are shown a wagon train gathering and preparing to set out on the Oregon Trail. Everything that occurs will be against this historical backdrop. The light-hearted nature of the romantic relationship between Coleman and Ruth Cameron is quickly established through the traditional comic device of mistaken identity (Coleman kisses her thinking she is somebody else). Tzvetan Todorov suggested all narratives followed a common pattern of movement from stable equilibrium to disruption to a reordered equilibrium and, essentially, a stable, balanced community space is what is initially given to us in this film. It is only when we are given a flashback to Old Ben's being found murdered that this balance is disturbed. As the hero, Coleman's task in Todorov's terms is to restore some sense of balance to the society.

Standard Western characters are found in both films; both heroes, for example, have a 'love interest.' Laura Lee (Sandra Locke) in The Outlaw Josey Wales fulfills a classic female role in helping the hero find his way back to a point where he is again able to both give and receive love. Ruth Cameron (Marguerite Churchill) in The Big Trail is involved in one of the most common narrative structures, a love triangle, formed in this case with Coleman and a stereotypical, smart-dressing gambler from the South. There are differences in the roles of these women within the narrative structures of the two films but also strong similarities. Although the role of welcoming the hero back into the community through tender physical contact is indicated rather than being so fully displayed as in The Outlaw Josey Wales, it is to the embrace of Ruth Cameron that Breck Coleman returns after having finally hunted down the villains. The 'final kiss'[47] that we have between Coleman and Cameron symbolically functions as the love scene between Wales and Lee, a tender return to a place where it is possible to appreciate the softer, feminine side

Figure 3.12   Pioneering families (*The Big Trail*, 1930)

of life. The endings are very different: whereas *The Big Trail* has a classic 'happy ending' with the hero returning to his love, as Josey Wales rides off toward the sunrise it is down to the audience to decide where he is going, further West or back to the homestead he has helped to set up with Laura.

Both Breck Coleman and Josey Wales have what in narrative terms might be called a quest that they are undertaking, or a goal they wish to achieve. Both reach this point with the death of the villain(s), killed at the climax to each film. Both have helpers who assist them in their venture but who cannot help in the ultimate task that has to be the hero's alone. Both can only be free from the burden upon them by following their quest through to its final conclusion. Both could be said to undertake a journey during the course of the film, but only Wales could really be said to change and develop as a character during the course of that journey. Wayne as Coleman travels most of the way across America but is so confident in himself and his beliefs from the outset that he remains unchanged by his experiences. Essentially, as is usual in storytelling, problems and conflicts set up early in the film are resolved after having reached a climactic moment of confrontation. Often, this operates as a means of confirming social norms and accepted consensual values. However, some matters may be left unresolved. That is, they may remain problematic, although apparently contained within the structure of the narrative. Ruth Cameron's plea to Breck Coleman as he resolutely sets out to kill the murderers of 'Old Ben' ('You can't do this awful thing and take two lives.'), for example, remains unresolved.

Both films have what could be seen as a further narrative interwoven with their key narrative of 'revenge.' Wayne as Coleman has the additional goal of guiding a wagon train along the Oregon Trail to a land of plenty, a place that is described when they get there as 'this valley of our dreams.' Eastwood as Wales also ends up with the task of guiding a small band of misfits to a better land in the West. Both face a series of conflicts and problems along the way as they move toward achieving these further goals (against 'Indians' but also in The Big Trail spectacularly against the forces of nature). So important is this 'secondary' narrative to The Big Trail that the personal narrative of Coleman's revenge is often subsumed beneath it. Perhaps the most important single speech in the entire film relates to this strand of the narrative as, in the face of a blizzard, Coleman reminds the pioneers of their historic role:

> We're blazing a trail that started in England … We've got to suffer: no great trail was ever blazed without hardship.

The film itself is dedicated to 'the men and women who planted civilization in the wilderness and courage in the blood of their children,' and the most powerful visual image is of a child wrapped in a blanket being buried in the foreground of a shot as a way of showing the suffering of crossing the desert. Similarly, in The Outlaw Josey Wales, key ideological points for the filmmakers are made in the 'secondary' narrative. As Wales secures peace with the 'Indians' for his pioneering band, he asserts: 'I'm saying that men can live together without butchering each other.'

The narratives of both The Big Trail and The Outlaw Josey Wales show a controlling order's being imposed on an imagined series of events. This controlling of events (so that, for example, the hero triumphs and love is achieved between the hero and his love-interest) gives meaning to the narrative. As we watch, we are reassured that any events that happen are not random, that all is not chaos, and that, ultimately, the world is a place of order and meaning, shape, and significance. As viewers who are already familiar with the storytelling conventions of Westerns, we approach these narratives with definite expectations. We expect to encounter characters from within a certain range of types, and we expect to find them involved in a series of structured events that occur in certain types of places and at certain historical times. So, in *The Big Trail*, events such as the wagon train's setting out, the buffalo hunt's taking place, the entrance into an Indian village, the circling of the wagons against the Indians, and the building of log cabins in the lush valley are all part of the range of possible narrative scenes we might expect to see. In this sense, narrative is intimately related to genre. Prior experience of the genre will be responsible for a major component of audience expectation.

Narratives can be seen as taking not just the central character but the viewer (or reader, or listener) on a journey. The plot engages the spectator in the creation of expectations, and these expectations are immediately fulfilled, delayed in their fulfillment, or cheated. When Terrill (Bill McKinney) burns down our hero's home in the opening to *The Outlaw Josey Wales*, we expect our hero to take revenge: this may take place immediately or may be postponed to some later date. However the storyline is structured because of our knowledge of the way narratives work, we have no choice but to actively engage in attempting to make logical narrative sense of what is unfolding. We are complicit with the creative storytelling act; we willingly engage in the process, giving of ourselves both emotionally and intellectually. A complex reading process is taking place; we are continually being expected to take up new perspectives, engage in new understandings, and shift our position in relation to new information. As viewers, we are (in this sense at least) active, and narrative depends upon this active interaction between text and reader.[48] Throughout the process, we are continually examining what has just happened. On the basis of our comprehension of each event within the context of the chain of events that have so far unfolded, we ask questions about what is likely (based on our previous experience of similar narratives) to happen next.

One of the functions of a narrative may be to deliver certain gratifications to us as an audience. Films must give us pleasure. We may be 'pleasured,' for example, by subconsciously knowing Todorov's narrative pattern and seeing it unfold before us; seeing, for example, Breck Coleman returning to the re-balanced community at the end of *The Big Trail*. We are gratified by having our expectations confirmed but also from existing within the tension of wondering whether our expectations will be fulfilled or undercut; thinking Coleman and Cameron will 'get together' but not knowing whether they will or not until the end of the film. We are 'pleasured' by the surprise of a new and unexpected twist that we are now able to add to our 'back-catalogue' of expectations. It seems that Josey Wales must take part in one final shoot-out as he steps into the street to stand opposite Fletcher (John Vernon), but then they talk and essentially negotiate an understanding, something that is decidedly not the Western norm. Roland Barthes suggested narrative worked through enigmas, the setting up of mysteries for the reader to solve. Again, the idea is that this is a process by which pleasure is provided for the reader. The mystery of what is going to happen between Wales and Fletcher has been something we have been trying to decide, and here the puzzle is solved for us in an unexpected way.[49]

WESTERNS AND REALISM

Focus films: *The Ox-Bow Incident* (William Wellman, 1943, 20th Century Fox) and *The Wild Bunch* (Sam Peckinpah, 1969, Warner Brothers / Seven Arts Productions).

We frequently talk about 'realism' in relation to film but usually employ the term without really considering what it might mean. We could define realism as a set of codes and conventions that have been given some cultural primacy within photographic and cinematographic representations. The advent of the camera brought about for the first time the opportunity to use a machine to 'simply' visually record what was 'out there' in the world. However, the camera is no more than another means of representing the world to an audience, and the images it produces depend on the input of the camera operator and editor. Whether we are drawing, painting, or using a camera, any final, definitive reality (whatever it may be) cannot be captured; it is forever elusive and can be given only particular interpretations that will offer insights into the human experience and may cast light on the nature of 'reality.'[50] From early in the history of cinema, in addition to attempts to reproduce 'actuality,' fantasy scenarios were constructed using cameras. Much of Edwin Porter's *The Great Train Robbery* (1903) might be said to employ realism but when, at the end, a gun is apparently pointed at the audience and fired, it is apparent that cinematic trickery is at work. The use of special effects more recently, as with the use of slow-mo in the final bloody shootout in *The Wild Bunch*, makes it clear that filmmakers and audiences have remained interested in the fantastical possibilities of film.

In overall terms, how should we judge Westerns as a genre in relation to notions of realism? The frequent allusions that are made to actual features of the late-nineteenth-century American past can be taken to imply that historically realistic scenes are being presented. The extent to which this is true will vary from film to film (and according to our understanding of American history of the period – one person's 'realism' is another person's fictional fantasy).[51] *The Wild Bunch* with its references to automobiles, airplanes, and machine guns, conveys a sense of the United States in 1913 as a period of change and gives an indication of the brutal chaos of the period in Mexico. And yet, the events that take place in the film are often fantastical, the coincidences implausible, the outcomes unlikely, and the tangled interweaving of character storylines unbelievable. In other words, the story has been carefully structured to create a particular narrative shape and order out of the chaos of reality. In this sense, rather than realism, what we have on offer in *The Wild Bunch* and in Westerns as a whole is clearly fantasy – an intense, dramatic representation of reality.[52]

Still, it remains true that Westerns frequently lay claim to various types of realism: not only historical realism but social realism and psychological realism, for example. *The Ox-Bow Incident* might not appear to be offering its audience any sort of realism as it is mostly shot on set with painted backdrops and, yet, we might argue the claustrophobic atmosphere that is achieved as a result of this is in some way realistic, perhaps giving a sense of psychological realism. The pursuit, capture, and lynching of the three men accused of killing Kincaid take place at night and so it is naturally dark, but the noir lighting goes beyond naturalism[53] to reinforce the psychological realism. Yet, there are moments in this film that might be said to employ naturalism. Before the posse moves down to capture the three sleeping men,

Figure 3.13   The looming presence of the lynching (*The Ox-Bow Incident*, 1943)

there is a drawn-out period of silence that feels as if it is taking place in real time during which the only sound is the men cocking their guns, one after the other. By contrast, just before this, there is a moment of sheer expressionism[54] as the entire posse is framed beneath the huge overhanging bough of a tree. At the same time, this shot moves toward symbolism with the tree moving beyond being a tree to the dark overhanging presence of what these men are about to do. Furthermore, when we begin to discuss symbolism, within a Christian context it seems likely the choice of having three men to hang is deliberate. We might, therefore, argue that several '-isms' operate alongside a range of realisms in a film such as *The Ox-Bow Incident* to create a complex matrix of interlocking styles.

When we use the term *reality*, we too often assume we know what is meant, but reality has no fixed meaning until it has been represented. Reality does not exist in terms of meaning until it has been represented. There is no final version of reality but only representations of reality, representations that will change over time and according to who is formulating them. The barroom brawl is a staple of the Western but an interesting thing happens in the fight in the saloon near the beginning of *The Ox-Bow Incident*: when Gil Carter (Henry Fonda) has his man down, he kicks him. A little later, when he comes round from being knocked out himself, he has to rush outside to be sick – in naturalistic terms, presumably because of the whisky he has drunk. These are perhaps minor points but, within the genre at the time, these are unusual additions to be made to the action. Over and against genre conventions, small but significant moves toward a particular understanding of realism are being made.

The real world does of course exist, but the meaning of the real world (or any element of the real world) exists only within representations. In using the term *reality*, the assumption is that there is some sort of 'out there' world that exists beyond the limits of our own personal world, the nature of which we can all agree upon. However, clearly the key question to be asked when we are confronted with any form of representation is whose version of reality is on display? It may be we are being directly given the filmmakers' version of reality, or it may be that the filmmakers are asking us to interpret their understanding of this through presenting us a version of reality that belongs to a narrator within their story. Our understanding of potential meaning within the story will depend upon who we see as being responsible for the storytelling. Who narrates the film story, from what perspective, and with what sense of detachment from or involvement in the events will each be key issues in the creation of meaning. William Wellman as director, along with others creatively responsible for the film, gives us a distinctive version of reality in *The Ox-Bow Incident*. Certain elements of the historical (but also the contemporary) American 'reality' are emphasized. The single African American, Sparks, for example, is laughed at by the townspeople making up the posse but is clearly given his own dignity by the filmmakers and (significantly) a high moral standing within the film.[55] The South is often idolized in Westerns, but this character is able to give a different sense of the 'reality' of that place:

I seed my own brother lynched, Mr Carter. I wasn't nothin' but a little fella but sometimes now wakes up dreamin' about it.

He is in many ways a typically subservient black character but with a telling freedom to speak his mind and act for himself. The other character associated with the South, Major Tetley (Frank Conroy), is a fraud who probably didn't fight in the Civil War, according to Carter. His son's final opinion of him is that

There are only two things that have ever meant anything to you, power and cruelty. You can't feel pity. You can't even feel guilt.

Yet, it seems he is the one member of the posse who takes ultimate responsibility for his actions and commits suicide. Where do we find the reality of Tetley as a character? Is this final action a contradiction of what his son has just said? Does this leave us with uncertainties about him? And, if so, is the sense of contradiction and uncertainty a form of realism?[56] Carter, we might note, is by no means a classic hero: despite his honest sentiments, he is powerless to save the three men. The only goal he can achieve is to save himself from the same fate. Is this a further example of realism?[57]

Our understanding of any film is going to depend upon how we interpret the version of reality with which we are confronted. To what extent could we say *The Ox-Bow Incident* presents us with the reality of lynch law in the West, and to what extent is it a distorted, or biased, representation of that historical reality that is shown to us? A version of reality is being offered, but how are we to judge its 'correctness' (or 'realism') if there is no single version of history but only a series of histories told from different perspectives and no final reality but only a series of realities. Certainly a perspective is being given: it is, for example, not the naturalism of three bodies hanging from a tree with which we are presented after the lynching but the symbolic expressionism of three shadows swinging on ropes, an altogether more powerful statement. Perhaps this could even be seen as some higher form of 'realism.' The choice of film noir style not only forces us to see the darkness of what has just occurred but confronts us with the darkness at the heart of man and, in doing so, the filmmakers achieve a realism that is beyond naturalism.

All narratives depend upon the selection of material and, therefore, by definition they must involve exclusion and inclusion. *The Wild Bunch*, for example, chooses to include images of children at every opportunity. One of the suggestions seems to be that children (destined to develop into the brutal adults populating the main narrative) are either already innately violent or at least quickly pick up violence from what they see around them. The film opens with images of the pleasure children seem to derive from watching ants swarm over two scorpions. Children gather round the dead bodies in the main street after the initial shoot-out and play out what they have just seen, seemingly immune to the gore with which they are

Figure 3.14   The 'education' of children (*The Wild Bunch*, 1969)

surrounded. Pike is finally killed by a boy-soldier. Is this an aspect of reality and a way of enhancing the realism of the film? Or are the filmmakers exaggerating or distorting reality? The nature of violent death is presented in this film with a certain realism that was previously unusual for the genre.[58] But, again exaggeration is also being employed in a way that moves the famous opening and closing sequences beyond realism.

WESTERNS AND AUTEUR THEORY

Focus films: *Winchester '73* (Anthony Mann, 1950, Universal), *Bend of the River* (Mann, 1952, Universal) and *The Man from Laramie* (Mann, 1955, Columbia/William Goetz Productions).

The concept of the 'auteur' emerged in France in the late 1940s–early 1950s when critics began to suggest there were certain directors who took such creative control over the films they were involved with as to leave their distinctive stamp on them. It was argued that this effectively made these directors the 'author' of the films. The special status of auteur was accorded to directors such as Orson Welles and Jean Renoir because of the 'signature' marks to be found across the range of films they made. Directors such as these were seen as working at a higher level of creativity than those who were more workman-like and simply put scenes together without imbuing the results with anything of their own personal vision.

Alexandre Astruc suggested in an essay on *la caméra-stylo* (the camera-pen) in 1948 that the auteur 'writes with his camera as the writer writes with his pen' (1967: 23). The term was used more provocatively in an article by Francois Truffaut, 'Une certaine tendance du cinéma français,' in the magazine *Cahiers du Cinema* (*Cinema Notebooks*) in 1954 in which he put forward the idea of the 'politique des auteurs'. This amounted to an artistic stance on how filmmakers should approach filmmaking and formed the basis of what in the 1960s became 'auteur theory.' Through the use of a unique, identifiable style, certain directors working within Hollywood, such as Howard Hawks, John Ford, and Sam Fuller, were said to have left their mark on a body of work. Despite the strictures of the Hollywood system of production, directors such as these were said to have been able to give a distinctive signature to their work.[59] The concept was subsequently extended to include the idea that certain stars, studios, or production teams working together over a period of time could be said to achieve the same sense of there being a distinctive unity of theme and style attaching to their work.

Here, we will consider three Westerns directed by Anthony Mann in the early 1950s to illustrate the possibilities of this approach within the context of genre. Two further films, *The Naked Spur* (1953) and *The Far Country* (1955), made by the same director in the same period could be used by anyone wanting to extend the analysis. Essentially, we will be looking for recurring themes, types of character, narrative structures, and filmmaking techniques that together might be said to produce a unity of form and outlook that could be attributed to the director's having exerted a controlling vision.

Each of these films at some point in the narrative has a central male character relentlessly pursuing another man to bring him to 'justice.' Lin (James Stewart) is a driven man tracking his brother in *Winchester 73* ('We been chasing him since before I can remember,' says his side-kick, 'High Spade'). In *Bend of the River*, Glyn (James Stewart) makes his intentions darkly clear to Cole (Arthur Kennedy):

> You'll be seein' me. Every time you bed down for the night you'll look back into the darkness and wonder if I'm there. And one day I will be. You'll be seein' me.

Stark shots frame Stewart standing awkwardly on a rocky hillside as he prepares to begin to follow Cole and in a similar position on rocky hillside as Will in *The Man From Laramie* (although this time on horseback) as he begins the pursuit of Vic (again, Arthur Kennedy).

In the first two films, the pursuit is made more poignant by Stewart's 'hunting' in the first film a brother and in the second someone akin to a brother. In *Winchester 73*, one brother, 'Dutch' Henry Brown (Stephen McNally), has killed his father, and this death has to be avenged by the other son. In *Bend of the River*, Glyn and Cole initially bond as 'brothers' by each saving the other's life, but eventually Glyn has to kill Cole. By the time of *The Man From Laramie*, the patriarch, Alec Waggoman, has not only a son, Dave (who even as an adult is treated as a child by his father) but what amounts to a foster-son, Vic. This shifts the central narrative focus away from the brother-on-brother emphasis of the first two films but allows for greater emphasis of the father–son relationship also found in the two earlier films. The end of *Bend of the River*, for example, has Glyn effectively being adopted by the organizer of the wagon train who becomes a father-figure, Jeremy Baile (Jay C. Flippen) and his wife, Marjie (Lori Nelson). Vic, the foster-son in *The Man From Laramie*, emphasizes the importance of these father–son relationships to Mann's narratives, saying to his 'father,'

> I was the only son you ever had but you couldn't see me ... I loved you like only a boy who never had a father could.

Male relationships are given a further focal point in male friendship bonds. In *Winchester 73*, High Spade accompanies Lin at every point of his journey, leaving him only to complete the final task of killing his brother on his own. Charley (Wallace Ford) fulfills a somewhat similar role in relation to Stewart's character in *The Man From Laramie* and, in *Bend of the River*, Trey (Rock Hudson) takes up this role after Cole has moved from friend/'brother' to enemy/'brother.'

Within all of this focus on male figures, narrative oppositions are set up between weak and strong men, and displays of cowardice and courage. Steve (Charles Drake) shows the struggle of a man to face up to his fear in *Winchester 73*. Dave (Alex Nicol) in *The Man From Laramie* is presented (and frequently described) as weak, but he also takes us toward a further recurring concern of Mann's: that of a violence in men that is associated with madness. A period of quiet within the film is torn apart for the viewer by Dave's suddenly burning the central character's wagons and shooting his mules, for example. Later, the same character has Stewart as Will held by his men as he shoots him in the hand from point blank range. In *Winchester 73*, Waco Johnny Dean (Dan Duryea) is played with a manic laugh and 'Dutch' Henry with a snarl constantly on the edge of his mouth. In *Bend of the River*, the dark edge to the character of the hero is displayed. Glyn is prevented from knifing a man only by a scream from Laura that draws him back from the edge, the moment being highlighted by the use of a close-up to show the utter brutality on Stewart's face. Crucially though, the hero is perhaps (in the terms set up by the films) able to draw the line between necessary and unnecessary violence. In *Bend of the River*, Glyn sets up a cold-blooded ambush of the wagon train's pursuers but then at a certain point calls to Trey and Cole: 'Alright, they've had it, let 'em go.' The reply from both men of 'Why?' receives the retort, 'Well, if you don't know, I can't tell you.' Trey stops shooting at this point, as if he understands, but Cole continues to fire.

The nature of man is, therefore, continually explored in these films; although the analysis may not always be very penetrating: 'Some things a man has to do, so he does 'em,' says Lin in *Winchester 73*. The concern in *Bend of the River* is that human nature is fixed and a man cannot change. In shooting his way out of town in an effort to obtain supplies for the wagon train community, Glyn threatens to become what he was in the past, a brutal Missouri border raider, and the concern is that Jeremy's metaphor ('When an apple's rotten there's nothin' you can do 'cept throw it away or it'll spoil the whole barrel.') is accurate. The madness that threatens individuals is also seen as capable of taking over entire communities, so that the gold rush boom-town in *Bend of the River* becomes a place of demented greed and self-interest. And in *The Man From Laramie*, Will has to remind Barbara,

> My coming here had nothing to do with the trouble here. The seeds of it were planted long before I ever heard of Coronado.

Women in these films often have to be stripped of romantic notions[60] and learn about men. Lola in *Winchester 73* has to find out about the weakness

Figure 3.15   On the edge of brutality (*Bend of the River*, 1952)

of Steve to come to appreciate the quiet strength of Lin. Laura in *Bend of the River* has to be brought to a position to see the brutal selfishness of Cole before she can appreciate the quiet, upright honesty of Glyn. Barbara in *The Man From Laramie* has to see the dark side to Vic before she can appreciate the strength of Will Lockhart.

To be able to explore these central thematic concerns, Mann employs a series of techniques. The rugged terrain of the West, for example, is a feature of the genre but is used here to suggest the harsh nature of the journeys being undertaken by characters and the brutality of the relationship between characters. The final shoot-out between Lin McAdam and 'Dutch' Henry in *Winchester 73* takes place on a rocky outcrop within dry, desert-like scenery. In *Bend of the River*, Glyn has to take the supply train up and over the mountains, facing harsh physical difficulties but also moral temptation as he is offered inflated prices by gold prospectors for the settlers' goods. The landscape continually tests the central characters and expresses the difficulty of their psychological journeys.

Men on horseback are often tracked as silhouetted outlines along a dark skyline, as with Lin McAdam and High Spade arriving in Dodge City in the early morning in *Winchester 73*. Film noir-style lighting like this is used both for outside scenes that frequently seem to take place in the early morning or evening, if not at night, and for interior locations. This gives expression to the darkness of the moral worlds of various characters and, more significantly, to the darker side of the central character's nature as in a fight in a hotel

Figure 3.16   Harsh landscapes (*Winchester 73*, 1950)

room in *Winchester 73* involving Stewart as the hero. When the hero, Will Lockhart (James Stewart), in *The Man From Laramie* finds somebody has been tracking him, he ambushes them and threatens them and, as he does, he is filmed with his hat casting an ominous shadow over his eyes. Much of this third film in particular is played out with the use of heavy shadows. Man's ability to descend into utter brutality is a central theme expressed in words and actions but also through the lighting. In *Winchester 73*, 'Dutch' Henry Brown filmed at night in the dark interior of an isolated bar threatens a gun trader by using an oblique suggestion that his family might be at risk if he doesn't come up with a deal:

I might even get one (a gun) that was meant to kill a white woman and her kids.

In these films, Mann uses close-ups to direct the audience's attention, as happens when we are shown the Winchester rifle on the gun trader's horse in *Winchester 73* a moment before Young Bull grabs it. (This could also operate as a point-of-view shot.) More significantly, he uses the close-up to direct attention to moments of fear, decision, or clarity coming across a male character's face. For instance, as Waco Johnny Dean trips Steve in *Winchester 73*, he falls toward the camera and into a close-up of his face that has his antagonist framed behind his right shoulder. The performance of Charles Drake as Steve, which the close-up forcefully presents us, makes it clear that this is a turning point.

Figure 3.17   Ominous shadows (*The Man from Laramie*, 1955)

Mann also employs shots from behind the hero in these films, realizing that the set of the back allied to the audience's own imagined interpretation of the look on the character's face can create its own power. The crouched body of Stewart as Glyn shot from behind as those opposing him take over the supply wagons in *Bend of the River* suggests an animal at bay but prepared to instantly spring into attack. The solid upright back of Young Bull (Rock Hudson) in *Winchester 73* is used in a different way. He jumps across in front of the camera, preventing us from seeing the death of the gun trader but creating a clear impression of threat that activates our imagination.

Silence is also used to create specific effects within the imagination. In *Winchester 73*, a period of silence taken beyond what would normally be expected in a Hollywood film of the time forces the audience to anticipate the impending Indian attack. In *Bend of the River*, when two men leave camp to find Glyn and kill him, we don't follow them but stay with the men in the camp listening to the silence until we hear, first one shot, and then after a further wait, a second shot, and the men fail to return.

Mann does employ common genre themes and stereotypes: the couple with the 'American dream' of living together on a ranch (Lola and Steve in *Winchester 73*); the gun-runner happy to trade with Indians (Joe Lamont in *Winchester 73* and Vic Hansboro in *The Man From Laramie*); the chase by Indians (Steve and Lola in a buckboard in *Winchester 73*); saving the last bullet (Lola in *Winchester 73*); and Civil War references (Glynn and Cole as Missouri border raiders in *Bend of the River*). He does use commonplace narrative structures such as the love triangle: Steve-Lola-Lin in *Winchester 73*, Cole-Laura-Glyn in *Bend of the River*, and Vic-Barbara-Will in *The Man From Laramie*. He does use common Hollywood themes such as seeing women as a symbol of home and family: in, for example, the shot of a mother embracing her two children in *Winchester 73* or Barbara in *The Man From Laramie* immediately being placed in the context of a drawing room with cups and saucers. So, to what extent does the genre allied to Hollywood expectations of narrative and thematic expression dictate the films being created here? Does Mann impose his personal vision and approach sufficiently for him to be seen as an auteur?

Furthermore, if there is something distinctively different happening in these films, is Mann really solely responsible for the themes and approaches to be found? The same star, James Stewart, is employed in all three. To what extent does his style of performance contribute to the final product? Is everything about that performance chosen by Mann and directed by him, or is Stewart responsible for the performative interpretation of character with which we are presented? Borden Chase is involved in writing the screenplays for both *Winchester 73* and *Bend in the River*. Are the themes found in these films in some way his rather than Mann's? Do the themes change in some way in the third film, *The Man From Laramie* and, if so, to what extent is this because of the involvement of Philip Yordan in the screenwriting?[61]

Stephen Neale (1980: 8) suggested the concept of an 'auteur' was inappropriate in relation to commercial cinema because the working conditions within the mainstream industry did not allow the necessary control over the final product. Certainly, one danger with an approach along the lines of the 'auteur theory' is that we are pushed toward assuming the film is simply a way for us to observe the workings of the director's mind. The film that we see in the cinema should be understood as the product of much more than this. To begin with, there is clearly a range of different people involved in constructing a film. Centrally, the process might be said to involve the producer, scriptwriter, cinematographer, and leading actors in addition to the director. However, any examination of film production will also reveal the involvement of a host of other workers and in addition make it clear that this is not only an aesthetic collaboration but an industrial process. The extent to which collaboration is allowed to occur will, of course, vary from film to film, as will the numbers of people involved in the process and the industrialization of that process.

WESTERNS AND STAR THEORY

Focus films: _Red River_ (Howard Hawks, 1948, United Artists/Monterey Productions) and _True Grit_ (Henry Hathaway, 1969, Paramount).

Stars are a key element in the organization of the film industry. For one thing, they offer a way in which products can be sold as a recognizable brand and, as such, play a key role within marketing. Through their media exposure, including past films they have made, stars will have acquired a certain image that audiences will expect to see reinforced in subsequent films. In ideological terms, any specific star could challenge a society's current dominant pattern of attitudes, values, and norms or, more likely, through their roles (and media persona) work to reinforce that status quo.[62] From this perspective, stars can be seen not as individual people but as sites at which a struggle takes place between ideologies and within ideologies. The constructed image of the star will be likely to deny the legitimacy of oppositional perspectives on society but may on occasions promote alternative ways of looking at the world.[63] John Wayne's star image was perhaps a powerful means of reinforcing dominant ideas of the macho male during the 1940s and 1950s. The image of Montgomery Clift (who acts opposite Wayne in _Red River_) contributed during the late 1940s and 1950s toward the creation of a more vulnerable male image.

Dominant star images and the meanings stars embody for a society may vary from one historical period to another. In this sense, stars may be seen to be in tune in some way with prevailing attitudes and ideas during their key years as stars. By the late 1960s and _True Grit_, the Wayne star image may have passed its 'sell-by-date' for many among the cinema-going public, despite the fact that the values embodied by his media-constructed self may well have continued to be in tune with a sizeable proportion of public opinion. A crucial question for a star-driven approach to film will be to decide how the constructed image of any given star relates to the struggle over social values at work within a society at a specific historical moment. Wayne is often seen as addressing a crisis in traditional masculine values and an uncertainty about the U. S. role in the world, whereas Montgomery Clift and others (such as Marlon Brando) in their roles in the 1950s can be viewed as expressing the oppositional values of youth culture developing in the '50s. In this sense, Wayne's star image is an attempt to bolster old values at a time when they are under increasing pressure. Or, perhaps it is more complex than this, and the Wayne star-image in any particular film might be seen to be more problematic than this allows.

The very name of the second film under consideration here, *True Grit*, highlights exactly what Wayne as star is about to portray in his role as 'Rooster' Cogburn. Mattie Ross (Kim Darby) is looking for a man who embodies 'true grit' to find her father's killer. Wayne as Cogburn is an old man holding to the old-time (mythic) Western values. The world around him has gone soft on the 'baddies' in his view, as he explains to Mattie:

> You can't serve papers on a rat, baby sister: you gotta kill him or let him be.

This may be the historic world of the West as it loses its title of 'wild' and becomes more 'civilized,' but it may equally be America of the late 1960s. Growing social unrest created largely as a result of the war in Vietnam and growing African American militancy brought into question conservative values and beliefs.[64] The idyllic world (or myth) that is at stake is made apparent from the beginning of the film as we open with a view of a homestead in a green valley with mountains in the distance. In this film, as heroic as the young Texan marshal, 'La Boeuf' (Glen Campbell), may be, he is ultimately not up to the job of dealing with the presence of evil in the world in the way that the 'one-eyed, fat man,' Cogburn, clearly is. The black hat and shirt and red necktie we initially see Cogburn wearing (and the noirish shadows across his face and eyes at various other points) suggest his

Figure 3.18   A 'one-eyed fat man' (True Grit, 1969)

dark side and the bloody violence of that dark side. He may need help from
'La Boeuf,' who saves his life at one point, but there is no doubting Wayne
is the hero of the film. He embodies courage, a ruthless determination to
bring 'justice' to lawless regions, and an instinctive willingness to support
the victim against the bully, the weak against the strong. This makes the
character of Cogburn a perfect fit for the star image of Wayne as displayed
not only in previous films but in other media, such as newspaper and
magazine articles.[65] However, at the same time as emphasizing key aspects
of Wayne's known star image, it may be that the eye patch worn by Cogburn
suggests someone who is unable to see everything clearly. Certainly Cogburn
is also an outsider in the mold of Ethan Edwards from The Searchers. He has
no family and no real place that society at large would recognize as a 'home.'
There would even seem to be some playing with Wayne's media-presented
persona happening here. The only place he has that approaches anything
like home is the back-room of a shop owned by a Chinese man. The only
leisure recreation he seems to have is playing cards with this Chinese man.
Additionally, he is frequently given lines belittling Texas and Texans. Wayne's
personal opposition to Chinese communism was well-documented, and
he was a famous advocate of what he saw as Texan values that were at the
ideological heart of his version of patriotic Americanism. In Westerns in a
Changing America, 1955–2000, R. Philip Loy says: 'However one categorizes
Wayne's Westerns after 1965, one thing is certain. The values they offer

Figure 3.19   Father and son (*Red River,* 1948)

are strikingly different from those that increasingly dominated the work of Sam Peckinpah and Clint Eastwood' (2004: 154). This may be true, but the relationship of these films to the values of the United States in the period is more complicated than this suggests.

However, it is *Red River*, the earlier film of the two under discussion here, that provides a more problematic fit between Wayne's star image and the character being played. To the public, Wayne embodied the Western legend of the honest, upright, straightforward cowboy, but here he plays the role of a driven man with an obvious darker streak to his character. In a sense, this is in keeping with what is found in other Hollywood films of the period. Noir-like features are found in postwar films from a range of genres. However, Wayne as Tom Dunson seems to negotiate his way through this dark phase so that, by the end, he has been reassuringly restored to his former star image. The film ends with a fistfight between Wayne and Montgomery Clift, in the role of Dunson's adopted son, Matt, that moves from a realistic attack on the younger man to a light-hearted, classic Western, saloon-style brawl. The resolution phase of the narrative attempts to suddenly resolve the extreme tensions that have been building through the rest of the film.[66] The audience is momentarily comforted but is ultimately unlikely to be able to shake off the image of the brooding, menacing older man who has said he is going to kill his son.[67] Potentially, in 1948 this may be an image of a man attempting to relocate himself in relation to his family after the experience of war, but it could also be seen as the anger of an older generation unable to understand the changing values and attitudes of young people.

Sons confronting fathers is clearly a conflict with a lengthy history of cultural representation, but it is also a source of tension in a series of postwar Hollywood films. And it may be that in the dislocation between Wayne's star image and the character he is playing, social tensions within contemporary American society are being revealed. Matt notes on his return that Tom, although he hides it, is actually scared because he is up against something he can't immediately see embodied in an oppositional male who he can take on physically. Groot (Walter Brennan) notes in voice-over: 'Tom had changed: he'd always been a hard man, now he was harder.' Is this the inner conflict of men returning from war, wrestling with their own inner demons, turning a cold, hard face to those around them, and ultimately lashing out at those same people? Ultimately, such an interpretation is too simplistic. It does contain some potential truth, but the mythic status that cultural representations are capable of embracing means that *Red River* would operate just as powerfully as a father's attempting to deal with the unseen forces of economic collapse in 1930s America. What is demonstrated is that in certain circumstances, fathers can displace violence on to sons. Maybe this needs to be explored in terms of psychology and with regard to the fact that Wayne as star often exists in relation to the absence of a female partner (or is awkward and uneasy in potentially romantic relationships). Here, his character's love-interest is killed in an Indian attack on a wagon train early in the film. Essentially, he has failed to protect her.

Wayne is in fact rarely the hero who is able to deal with any situation. He is always strong and sincere in his beliefs and approach:

> I don't do much really, I suppose, just sell sincerity. And I've been selling the hell out of it ever since I got going.
>
> (Shipman, 1979: 563)

However, he frequently exists in relation to some failure to be the true classic hero. What he does have almost always is a dogged determination to pursue to the end a route he believes to be right.[68] It is often asserted that stars exist as a construct of all of their media expressions, that the articles about them and the interviews with them run alongside their film roles to create the star image, but it may be that during the period of his fame, Wayne as star existed for most people more simply as an amalgam of his film roles, the support for right-wing political positions that he gave outside of his film roles being insignificant in relation to the image constructed on screen over a period of more than 40 years.

Certainly, social tensions within the contemporary period in America are played out in the characters he plays (not least, perhaps, in relation to the unspoken issue of homosexuality). Certainly, the characters he plays can be seen as sites of ideological conflict. Yet, Wayne's star image is not an unproblematic expression of the dominant ideology that is working to deny the legitimacy of alternative or oppositional ideologies. It is too easy to see Wayne's star image as simply a powerful means of reinforcing dominant right-wing ideas.[69] There is always a struggle over the social values to be espoused in any society at any historical moment, and Wayne as star operates as one site for that struggle. Wayne can be viewed as (desperately) continuing to assert the importance of the heroic male and a resulting brand of American nationalism in the face of growing youthful opposition and setbacks suffered in American foreign policy, notably in Vietnam, but there's probably more to Wayne's star image (and the role of star images in general in society) than this allows. For one thing, audiences use the experience of films to their own ends, to negotiate perhaps their own response to what it means to be male. Star images will be seen differently by different individuals at different times and in different places: the image, and most of all what the image means, will be contested.[70]

WESTERNS AND PSYCHOANALYTICAL THEORY

Focus films: *Duel in the Sun* (King Vidor, 1946, Vanguard Films/Selznick Studio), and *Pursued* (Raoul Walsh, 1947, Warner Brothers/United States Pictures).

One form of psychoanalytical approach to Westerns, as with films in general, would be to consider them in relation to the viewing experience. This might involve seeing films as working to produce fantasies that feed the human desire to be 'complete.' Jacques Lacan suggested that from the moment of their birth, human beings were faced by a sense of loss, or 'lack.' He suggested an illusion of wholeness was obtained from being able to conceptualize a sense of the self 'out there' in the world. To explain this, he used the concept of the mirror, speaking of the 'mirror phase' of childhood development. Recognition of the 'out there' self was characterized as the moment of seeing the self in a mirror and recognizing it as oneself. Lacan suggested this was actually a moment of mis-recognition, as this image was neither complete (as it appeared to be) nor the 'real' self. This idea of the mirror phase can be compared to an act of spectatorship in which the viewer identifies with a character on the screen. We could speculate that in this act of spectatorship the viewer temporarily experiences some sense of wholeness.[71] From this perspective, one of the attractions of watching John Wayne or James Stewart in action is that we can momentarily see ourselves as them and gain some comforting (although ultimately fleeting) imagined sense of being 'complete.' Such an approach would seem to become more problematic if we begin to identify with more troubled characters such as those played by Gregory Peck and Robert Mitchum in the focus films under discussion here. It also raises the issue of whether it is the character or the star image that offers the critical focal point for identification. Furthermore, does identification with Jennifer Jones as Pearl in *Duel in the Sun* or Teresa Wright as Thorley in *Pursued* offer the same type of satisfaction, or sense of completion, for female spectators?

Leaving aside the issue of whether the screen can operate as something equating to the Lacanian 'mirror phase,' the act of viewing films still provides us with the pleasure of looking, or scopophilia. It seems to be the case that we receive some psychological pleasure in simply looking at others and in watching what happens to others. In everyday terms, this might be seen as human curiosity but, if so, this is a perspective on curiosity that suggests that it fulfills a deep-seated, human need. The related concept of voyeurism includes the idea of the additional (maybe sexual) pleasure gained from believing oneself to be looking at others as an unseen observer. Clearly, particularly as we watch alone or in the darkened cinema space, film offers this possibility, and Westerns often project larger-than-life characters with whom we might take pleasure in identifying as a form of self. In *Duel in the Sun*, Pearl often becomes the object of the male gaze, allowing the viewer to engage in a prolonged, voyeuristic look at various parts of her body. In *Pursued*, aided by Mitchum's distinctive use of voice and body that creates a performance that draws attention to itself, the camera tends to linger on him.[72]

An alternative psychoanalytical approach would be to focus more directly on the characters and character relationships within the film narrative. Sigmund Freud proposed a hidden dimension to life beneath our experience of surface 'reality.' His key insight was to suggest we each strive to fulfill our desires, especially sexual desires, while at the same time experiencing guilt for those desires. We each experience frustration when we are unable to fulfill our desires and self-disgust, or guilt, about having these desires. We repress these feelings of frustration and self-disgust into the unconscious, but eventually the 'repressed' re-emerges in some form. Furthermore, Freud said our instinctual 'drives' dictate much of what we say and do at the conscious level. Following this line of argument, psychoanalytical theorists have suggested that which is hidden, displaced, or repressed can be found within the 'sub-text' of a text. Could these insights offer a useful approach to narratives within Westerns? Certainly much of what is said here could be seen to relate directly to the character of Pearl in *Duel in the Sun*. The key insight offered by a psychoanalytical approach is to make us acutely aware of the fact that (as representations of ordinary people) every character, far from being a unified stable being, is in fact a complex matrix of contradictory drives and repressions.

Duel in the Sun was dubbed 'Lust in the Dust' by some when it was released. This expressed recognition of the way in which both the narrative and individual characters are driven by sexual desire. The burning reds and vibrant oranges frequently employed in the cinematography suggest passion but – more important – the heat of barely controlled (repressed) sexual energy. These burning colors are also linked to a sense of danger, a sense of sex as in some way dangerous, and this notion of danger links directly to the complementary use of noir-style darkness and shadows at other places in the film. At moments, characters are released, or defiantly release themselves, from the restrictive bonds of social sexual conformity. The opening focus on Pearl's mother dancing in the saloon and Pearl's replication of the dance outside displays women releasing themselves from social norms; dance allows a revelation of the sexuality held close beneath the surface of society. For Freud, our psyche is composed of the id, the repressed part of our psyche; the ego, or consciousness, which attempts to exert control over the id; and, the super-ego, which attempts to gain critical distance and understanding of the id and the ego. The realist ego mediates between the pleasure-seeking id and social norms, helping us to conform to society's expectations of our behavior. However, neither Lewt nor Pearl can bring their sexual desire into line with society's expectations. Lewt is the phallus embodied. At one stage, he is on the run but returns to Pearl's room at night, the sheriff and his posse move in, and it appears he may be captured: there is a shot that is almost entirely black apart from Lewt's gun fully lit in the centre and his half-lit face in the top right-hand corner.[73] Both Lewt and Pearl are outsiders, forced beyond the bounds of society by their willingness to express, or inability to control, their sexuality. Pearl wants to be what she describes as 'good' and berates herself as 'trash' because of her inability to live up to what is expected of a 'lady.'[74] Lewt enters the home on occasions and appears in town, but his natural environment is out on the range, roaming beyond the bounds of society. Neither character can be allowed to live. Jesse (Joseph Cotten) and his wife, Helen (Joan Tetzel),[75] want to tame Pearl, but she leaves to fulfill a final, violent, intensely

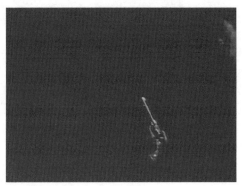

Figure 3.20   Lewt's gun (*Duel in the Sun*, 1946)

passionate coupling with Lewt. When she journeys toward Lewt for this final expression of their natures, she has taken possession of the phallus. She rides bareback as she has from the moment she was dared to do so by Lewt[76] and carries an upright, erect rifle by her side.[77]

Lacan suggested that beyond the mirror phase, the child gained entry into society, but this was at the expense of feeling divided and continuing to experience a sense of lack. When we acquire language, we are able to exist through it (as a name or as 'I'), and yet that existence is always something less than the 'I' who speaks. The society entered is one of masculine order and authority, which oppresses women. Women are constituted as subjects but exist within a symbolic order in which they are treated as objects; the woman is nothing in that she does not possess the phallus, and yet she is everything in that she is the terminus for desire. This might be said to fully express Lewt's attitude toward Pearl. What he wants, as he says, is to 'come back every once in a while and see you like tonight.'

Pursued is clearly about the ongoing childhood trauma of the central character, Jeb Rand (Robert Mitchum), who has witnessed his father's murder. Recalling the night of his father's death, Jeb says: 'I was in a dark, cold place. I had my eyes closed to get away from some bad dream, the same dream I've been havin' all my life. I have never understood it.' Scenes are constantly set either at night or in the evening, so that almost the entire film seems to take place in a 'dark, cold place.' Jeb is often seen

Figure 3.21 'I was in a dark, cold place' (Pursued, 1947)

within enclosed spaces or divided from other characters by intervening objects. Even in outdoor spaces, he is shown as a lone rider traversing difficult terrain against a backdrop of sheer rock faces. In line with basic psychoanalytical therapy, he has to return to his childhood memories to make sense of his life.

The family into which Jeb is adopted is a dysfunctional place with hidden, ultimately sexual secrets. Freud's concept of the Oedipal complex suggested the male child must be severed from its imaginary unity with the mother. The father had to intervene so that the child renounced (essentially, repressed) its desire for fear of castration. To complete the Oedipal trajectory successfully, the male child must then find its own female as reward for renouncing the mother. A girl, according to Freud, on discovering the mother's castration, can give up on sexuality because she cannot compete, seek the phallus for herself, or take the father as love object. Social taboos mean the girl must reject the father and seek substitute love objects.[78] Despite the absence of a father within the family unit, Grant Callum (Dean Jagger) does intervene as a father figure, shooting a horse from under Jeb when he is a young boy. Jeb moves on to find his female but takes her from within his family, displacing his love for the mother onto the daughter.[79] Thorley seeks the phallus but, again, from within the family (possibly, in a unit lacking a father, seeing Jeb as that father figure). Within this distorted version of the family, love is intense but has the capacity to transform itself into cold hatred. After Adam's death, Mrs. Callum says to Jeb: 'All the love I had for you is dead.' The passion of the relationship between Jeb and Thorley has the potential to play itself out in the same way as that between Lewt and Pearl.[80] However, in this film, it is the sex act of a previous generation that climaxes. Mrs. Callum takes the upright rifle (placed in the foreground of the shot) and kills the man whose repressed desire for her has set into play the whole narrative.

WESTERNS AND POSTMODERNISM

Focus films: *Blazing Saddles* (Mel Brooks, 1974, Crossbow/Warner Brothers) and *Buffalo Bill and the Indians, or Sitting Bull's History Lesson* (Robert Altman, 1976, United Artists/Dino De Laurentiis/Lions Gate/ Talent Associates).

In the late twentieth century, social theorists such as Jean-Francois Lyotard and Jean Baudrillard promoted the idea of the postmodern. Living in the contemporary period of postmodernity,[81] we were said to be experiencing the world in a new way, subject to what was described as the 'postmodern condition.' Has this new human experience been reflected in the making of Westerns, and could we use the concept of postmodernism to help us explore films that might be classified within the Western genre? Lyotard suggested the postmodern period was characterized by a loss of faith in old meta-narratives, or 'grand narratives,' such as Christianity and Marxism, that were once believed capable of explaining the world. As a result, the postmodern world was experienced in terms of discontinuity, fragmentation, and growing individual confusion. This may help to explain the decline in the numbers of Westerns being produced after 1970; a form that has been fundamentally based around a belief in agreed moral values and social norms shared between the producers of these genre films and the audience might naturally be expected to find difficulties moving into such a new space uncertainty.[82] At the conclusion of *Blazing Saddles* the hero, a black sheriff, says:

> My work here is done: I'm needed elsewhere now. I'm needed wherever outlaws rule the West, wherever innocent women and children are afraid to walk the streets, wherever a man cannot live in simple dignity, wherever a people cry out for justice.

To which the response of the simple folk of the fictional Western town of Rock Ridge is: 'Bullshit.' The inflated language of the Western is being exposed as empty hyperbole and, in the process, the entire genre is brought into question. However, beyond this, the moral confidence and assertiveness that saw grand, large-scale values such as honesty, truth, and justice as embodied in 'the American way of life' is demolished in one short, sharp response. In a similar way, in *Buffalo Bill and the Indians*, it is clear that Cody's power is bounded by the parameters of the circus-cum-rodeo within which he performs. The myth of the American way of life that he represents has no potency beyond the boundaries of show business. When Cody gathers a parody of a Western posse to pursue Sitting Bull, he too employs the inflated language of the Western genre. His female companion says in typical 'little-woman-left-at-home' style: 'How long will you be gone?' To which he replies, 'As long as it takes.' Of course, he returns totally worn out, having been completely unable to track Sitting Bull.[83]

The destruction of an American grand narrative (and the refusal to replace it by any new all-encompassing myth) is central to *Buffalo Bill and the Indians*. The film opens with the wind howling steadily, a view of mountains in the distance, and the American flag being raised over what appears to be a cavalry fort to the sound of a bugle. It presents itself as the opening to a Western in the classic style, but the comfortable certainty with which the audience relaxes into place before this spectacle is quickly undermined. It becomes clear that what we are witnessing is a fabrication, a performance, a show: in fact, Buffalo Bill's Wild West Show of 1885.[84] In revealing its own constructed nature, the film brings into question not simply the legend, or perhaps meta-narrative, of the 'American Frontier' but the myth at the core of the Western genre. Beyond this, the audience is being confronted with the constructed nature of all films. The filmmakers have employed classic genre signifiers to draw the audience into believing this film will

Figure 3.22   A black sheriff (*Blazing Saddles*, 1974)

conform to their genre expectations only to immediately turn the tables. All
the 'certainties' (of American legend, of the Western genre, of film itself)
that an audience sitting before the screen might expect to share with one
another and with the filmmakers have been taken away. The film is showing
us from the outset that all representations are constructed and that we are
surrounded by the inescapable human experience of storytelling. Having the
'Players' listed at the beginning of the film draws attention to the fact that
we are watching actors. Having their roles designated as 'types' (the Legend
Maker, the Producer, the Relative) further reinforces the point that what we
are witnessing is the acting of parts given to the 'players.' Further, the use of
the term *players* in itself places the storytelling that is to take place within a
long theatrical tradition.

We are presented with a show-within-a-show: the actors are playing
roles within Buffalo Bill's Wild West Show but are actually actors within a
film about that show. Further attention is, therefore, drawn to the 'acting'
and the 'constructedness' of what we are seeing. This foregrounding of the
falsity of the filmed 'illusion of reality' means the spectator is deprived of the
usual easy indulgence in comforting reassurances afforded by the cinema
experience and forced to confront the storytelling processes whereby the
world is represented to an audience. Burt Lancaster as 'the Legend Maker'
tells a group in a saloon how he found William Cody and made him into a
legend, whereas outside a wizened old actor (apparently) within the Wild
West Show tells a group of children the story of Buffalo Bill: both are telling
stories. And this would seem to be the point: all is storytelling. Additionally,
because our attention has been drawn to the film-making process, Lancaster

is unable to escape being the star, 'Burt Lancaster,' playing a role. We are acutely aware of Lancaster as star and as seen in a string of previous movies. This is even more strongly apparent to the spectator when viewing Paul Newman as Cody. He is designated on the roll of players as performing the role of 'the Star' and, indeed, he is a star of whose presence within the interlocking late-twentieth-century media we are well aware. As we have a show-within-a-show, so we have a star-playing-a-star. When Newman enters the arena on a white horse, because our attention has been drawn to the 'constructedness' of film, we do not enter into the illusion of its being Buffalo Bill Cody; instead, we see it as Paul Newman playing Buffalo Bill Cody. At the end of the film, there is a startling shot of the disembodied head of Newman-Cody in a mirror surrounded by blackness delivering the line: 'I got people with no lives living through me.'

Blazing Saddles similarly plays with audience expectation. It too draws attention to itself as a construct. In *Buffalo Bill and the Indians*, on the cue of 'From the beginning: one, two...' a band begins playing what the audience had initially taken to be soundtrack background music: In *Blazing Saddles*, Bart comes across a band in the desert playing what had appeared to be 'normal' background film music. As we move into the final 10 minutes of the film, the camera withdraws to a long shot and, from the privileged aerial position offered to the spectator, it is clear everything is taken place within the back-lot of Warner Brothers' Burbank Studios. We then find ourselves watching the filming of a musical, before the actors in the nominal Western we had been viewing previously crash through what turns out to be a false

Figure 3.23   Newman-Cody's disembodied head (*Buffalo Bill and the Indians*, or Sitting Bull's History Lesson, 1976)

dividing wall, and a fight breaks out between the two casts. The mayhem replicates the chaotic mixture of usually discrete film forms with which we are confronted. The comedy of the film had long been leading us to understand the 'characters' as actors within a film, and now the performative nature of film is fully confirmed. One of the features of the postmodern is said to be the way in which genres and past styles are recycled in an eclectic, undifferentiated mix, an inter-textual pastiche with no context over and above itself as representation. This would seem to be exactly what is happening here. Though still contained within the overarching concept of a film by Mel Brooks, the actors go on to break out from the Warner Brothers film 'factory' into the streets of Los Angeles. Bart (Cleavon Little) and Jim (Gene Wilder) end up entering a cinema to watch the ending to *Blazing Saddles*, the film they are supposedly in. Paralleling the structure of *Buffalo Bill and the Indians*, we have, rather than a show-within-a-film, something like a film-within-a-film, except that the logic of time sequence is also being disrupted because we are watching a film that logically has not yet been completed. The notion of 'play' would seem to be the essence of what is occurring in this film. Postmodernism 'plays' with form and with audience expectations, demanding a detached 'knowingness' of the spectator.[85] Similarly, *Buffalo Bill and the Indians*, although lacking the surreal comedy of *Blazing Saddles*, could be said to play with the audience's conceptions of film, of the Western, of the West and, ultimately, of 'America.' From an immediately more serious perspective, postmodernism questions the existence of any knowable reality outside of representation. And this might be said to be something like the understanding to which both of these films leads. Both may ultimately be said to be about the nature of representation and in particular about its inescapable all-pervasiveness within the human experience.[86]

There is also, according to Abercrombie (1996), a blurring of boundaries between cultures, between geographical locations and between historical periods, to be found in postmodernism. Place becomes all places without singularity, and time becomes a free-floating unspecified moment. In *Blazing Saddles*, as the 'desperate men' preparing to enter Rock Ridge and destroy the town line up to be signed on as hired guns, we find that besides the stereotypical 'low-life' characters of the Western genre, there are German paratroopers, Hells Angels, and Arabs on camels. In the eclectic mix of postmodernism, films genres and stereotypical characters exist in inter-textual relationship to each other. The character of Lili von Shtupp singing 'I'm Tired' is to some extent humorous in its own right but also exists in relation to the hallmark features of filmed performances by Marlene Dietrich. The cattle constantly appearing in rooms is a basic joke about Westerns but, in their surrealism, these moments echo the cow on the bed in Luis Bunuel's *L'Age d'Or*. Because we are aware of Newman-as-star in *Buffalo Bill and the Indians*, we cannot escape the face on the screen in *Butch Cassidy and the Sundance Kid* (1969) and a series of other movies including maybe even *The Towering Inferno* (1974)!

WESTERNS AND AUDIENCE RESPONSE

Focus films: *Johnny Guitar* (Nicholas Ray, 1954, Republic) and *Heaven's Gate* (Michael Cimino, 1980, United Artists/Partisan Productions).

In common with all media texts, films exist in relation to audiences. Audiences represent a key element in the industrial, commercial, and creative process as films are made to be paid for and consumed. *Heaven's Gate* was a notorious 'flop' when it was originally exhibited.[87] By the time it was ready to be shown, it had accumulated higher production costs – at more than $40 million – than any Hollywood film in the previous decade. The director's cut was poorly received at its premiere. It was then released in a shortened version, made less than $2 million at the box office, and consequently played a major role in the collapse of United Artists. Though it was not costly to make, *Johnny Guitar* was not well received when it came out. It was criticized as pretentious and for refusing to take the genre seriously.[88] Both films would, therefore, seem to have failed to connect effectively with their audience. And yet, both films have continued to attract considerable attention since their initial release, *Johnny Guitar* becoming something of a cult movie and the merits of *Heaven's Gate* frequently being assessed and reassessed.

Reflecting on any film in relation to audience response is an awkward process. Even suggesting spectators watching a film might form a sufficiently cohesive unit to be tagged an 'audience' is fraught with difficulty. Ultimately, each member of an audience brings his or her own unique, socially complex matrix of being to that experience. In the fully developed final analysis, we may be able to talk only of the relationship of a single unique reader to a particular film at a particular moment within a particular environment. However, there remains a sense in which the individual members of any audience can be seen as linked to one another through their shared experience of a particular film. Watching a film with others, we are joined through an act of viewing. Discussing a film with others, we assume some sense of a common viewing experience. Films such as *Johnny Guitar* and *Heaven's Gate* bring the relationship of text to audience particularly strongly to the fore.

In the production of Westerns, filmmakers (and the film industry) are constructing a text designed to elicit certain responses from the audience. They might also be attempting to encourage the audience to see the world in certain ways. In both instances, the effort is to exert some form of control over the audience's response to the film, but the audience is not necessarily easy to control. In the case of a strongly delineated genre such as Westerns, audiences are likely to bring a well-developed set of expectations with them to the viewing experience. This will clearly influence the way in which they respond to the film. Audiences might be excited by the various ways in which films such as *Johnny Guitar* and *Heaven's Gate* reinterpret the Western and attempt to reshape the possibilities of the genre, but equally they may find such reinterpretation and reshaping unacceptable.

Naturally, as audiences are made up of a diversity of people, it is likely they will respond in diverse ways to any film. Factors such as gender, ethnicity, class, sexual orientation, cultural background, and religious belief might be likely to affect the way in which films are viewed. At a basic level, it is likely an African American audience from the 1940s would view the performance of Hattie McDaniel in *They Died With Their Boots On* in a way different from that of an all-white audience. Similarly, members of an American audience able to trace their family roots back to Eastern Europe might respond in a distinctive way to representations of small-scale homesteaders in *Heaven's Gate*. A female audience might respond differently than a male audience to *Johnny Guitar* both in response to Joan Crawford as Vienna and to Mercedes McCambridge as Emma. However, it is also true that a genre film is selling a well-defined brand and, therefore, may be likely (initially, at least) to attract a more uniform body of viewers. Within a particular, more-clearly defined audience such as this, it is likely there will be some tendency to adopt common perspectives through the repeated absorption of similarly constructed texts. If the resulting outlooks of norms and expectation are strongly challenged, the audience is unlikely to accept the film. The audience will be resistive to the meanings and perspectives seen to be embedded in the text.[89]

Bearing these sorts of ideas in mind, it seems important to approach a film genre such as Westerns with an awareness of the way in which films come into social being through their relationship with audiences. In the period when the fictional James Averill (Kris Kristofferson) left Harvard in *Heaven's Gate* in 1870, having been urged to pursue the 'high ideal' of 'the education of a nation,' there would have been an assumption that the education on offer would be based on 'high culture' and grounded in the Classics.[90] The effort would be to raise people to what was seen as a higher level of civilization. The homogenous nature of the audience as classically educated scholars or those aspiring to this state was taken for granted. Low-brow reading material or other lower-class 'cultural' pursuits were not deemed worthy of serious consideration. By the time the film itself is made in 1980, this position has been seriously challenged; popular culture has come to be seen as being of interest in its own right, and it is recognized that novels, plays, and films, for example, can be viewed in a diversity of ways. As Averill moves beyond the walls of Harvard, an institution priding itself on sending its students into the world to do public service, he believes he is doing so as a superior being.[91] James becomes 'Jim' and takes up what in British colonial terms was seen as the 'white man's burden,' traveling into the interior of the country to bring the light of civilization.[92] Jim's attempt to bring something better to others fails, just as Michael Cimino's attempt to apply a more thoughtful approach to the Western and bring something different to the genre audience failed at the box office. Yet, because the audience for any film is not in fact singular but plural and − more than this − an evolving and changing plurality, *Heaven's Gate* has been the subject of continually contested re-evaluations.

Heaven's Gate is more than three-and-a-half hours long: *High Noon* is less than an hour-and-a-half, epic Westerns such as *Shane* and *The Searchers* are less than two hours, and even *Once Upon a Time in the West* is well shorter than three hours. The initial 20 minute section of the film is set in Harvard,[93] as far from a classic Western location as it is possible to get, and this opening is slow, rather static, and lacking in action. In terms of its structure, this Western is then extremely challenging to the genre audience. Just as damagingly, it undermines fundamental myths of the West. Class, and the economic basis to class, is never so clearly announced as the engine driving events on the frontier as it is here. Racial prejudice against white ethnic groups is never approached head-on as an issue in Westerns as it is here.[94] The notion of the West as a place where anyone from any origins could prosper if they were only prepared to work and face hardships − perhaps the key ideological theme of the Western − is destroyed.[95] The comfort enjoyed by members of the Stockgrowers' Association is made clear by the *mise en scène* in their club and is presented even more forcefully by being contrasted with the extreme poverty of the immigrants. Images from past Westerns of pioneers moving forward stoically but happily on wagons and horseback clash violently in the mind of the viewer with the heavy, trudging, head-bowed, mud-wracked progress of the huddled masses of immigrants with which we are presented here.[96] At every turn, in other words, the expectations of the experienced genre reader are challenged.[97]

The title *Johnny Guitar* seems to promise a story with a male main character, but Vienna is, in fact, most definitely centre stage. In narrative terms, Johnny 'Guitar' Logan (Sterling Hayden) is little more than the hero's helper. The final shoot-out is between two women, both of whom wear the male gun at various points through the film. As with *Heaven's Gate*, the audience's genre expectations are being undermined. Crawford's excessive performance means the predominantly male genre audience can never feel the female protagonist is being controlled and feminine sexuality contained (Robertson,

Figure 3.24   Huddled masses (*Heaven's Gate*, 1980)

1996: 105–109). Through a series of extreme costume changes, close-ups of her face lit as Hollywood star, and dramatic movements through the space of the action, Crawford's Vienna dominates the screen, imposing herself on the film and on the audience. When we first see her, she is dressed in black and wearing trousers and cowboy boots. Her first two main actions are to strap on a gun and then to draw that weapon. And yet, her face is heavily made-up and her red lipstick prominently displayed. If *Heaven's Gate* draws attention to the twin issues of class and economics, this film impacts most forcefully on the audience through its displays of sexuality. The struggle between the repression and the expression of female sexuality embodied in the antagonism between Emma and Vienna is at the heart of the film. Issues of ownership are here[98] – as issues of sexual independence are in *Heaven's Gate*[99] – but, in this instance, they are not what is driving the film. The final kiss, a classic element of the genre, attempts to reclaim the 'dominant male–subordinate female' social norm but is insufficient to counter-balance the weight of all that has gone before.[100]

Westerns need to be seen in relation to audience theory. At one time, mass audiences were seen as easily controlled and manipulated by the media: they are now generally seen as more able to take their own view on things. However, although the audience for any Western is potentially extremely diverse in terms of class, gender, ethnicity, sexuality, and ideology, it may be more homogenous than this suggests because of the shared genre focus. Potentially, heavy use of a particular genre might be expected to narrow

Figure 3.25   Joan Crawford as powerful woman (*Johnny Guitar*, 1954)

the range of opinions held by a viewer. Cultivation theory suggests it is the buildup of textual experiences over the long term that determines response; that is to say, given sufficient time and exposure to particular ways of seeing the world, certain responses can be cultivated within an audience. If we analyze the 'message-systems' employed by Westerns, we would find, for example, that certain roles are ascribed to men and women (and that certain screen-times are allocated to the two genders): what effect might this have on the audience? The findings of cultivation analysis warn us, however, that what we are dealing with here are tendencies rather than absolute certainties. Those who watch a lot of Westerns *may* tend to see things in a particular way or to think within certain narrow boundaries, but individuals are always likely to contradict these findings. In theory, audience members remain able to use films in their own way to achieve their own pleasures. Furthermore, particular films within a genre may work to thwart the expected pleasures of audiences employing common genre approaches.

NOTES

1. 'The major defining characteristics of a genre will be visual,' (Buscombe, 2003: 20).
2. 'Music, speech and sound effects are also powerful auditory signifiers of genre' (Gillespie and Toynbee, 2006: 53).
3. See Fujitani, White, and Yoneyama's *Perilous Memories: the Asia-Pacific War(s)* for a placement of this debate within the context of war (2001: 41).

4. See Ken Dancyger's *The Technique of Film and Video Editing: History, Theory and Practice* (2007: 116–118) for a slightly fuller consideration of Sturges's use of editing and cinematography.

5. See Ronald Lackmann's *Women of the Western Frontier in Fact, Fiction and Film* (1997: 52–59) for a clearer sense of the real historical women referenced in this film.

6. See the section on Westerns and Auteur Theory later in this chapter, pp. 84–92.

7. Notice although the film is about prejudice toward Japanese Americans, nobody from this ethnic background appears in the film, and it is a heroic white male who clears up the problem (see Benshoff and Griffin, 2004: 125).

8. Sturges is reported to have taken 44 hours to film the shoot-out (Murray, 2000: 24).

9. However, perhaps we should make sure we do not confine ourselves simply to a genre approach. If we do, we will, for instance, miss the wider historical significance of the 'Gunfight at OK Corral':

> Battles associated with legendary names such as Billy the Kid and Wyatt Earp were essentially the same sort of factional struggles for economic or political power that also marked the elections in contemporary New York City or Philadelphia (Jenkins, 2007: 158).

10. Semiotics, or semiology, is the study of meaning as inscribed within individual 'signs' as they operate within codes and conventions.

11. '... human culture is made up of signs, each of which stands for something other than itself, and the people inhabiting culture busy themselves making sense of those signs.' (Bal and Bryson, 1991: 174, quoted in Rose, 2007: 75.)

12. Barthes' classic example of how he saw 'the photographic message' as working records his response to an image on the cover of the magazine, *Paris Match*. 'I am at the barber's, and a copy of *Paris Match* is offered to me. On the cover, a young Negro in a French uniform is saluting, with his eyes uplifted, probably fixed on the fold of the tricolour. All this is the meaning of the picture. But, whether naively or not, I see very well what it signifies to me: that France is a great Empire, that all her sons, without colour discrimination, faithfully serve under the flag, and that there is no better answer to the detractors of an alleged colonialism than the zeal shown by this Negro in serving his so-called oppressors.' (Barthes, 1972: 125-126)

13. See Robert Stam's 'The Birth of the Spectator' in *Film Theory: An Introduction* (2000: 229–234) for a brief overview of the emergence of the concept of spectatorship in the 1970s.

14. This film, focusing on three Bonnell brothers working as U. S. marshals, is set in 1881. This is the year of the 'Gunfight at the OK Corral' that involved three Earp brothers working in a frontier town in Cochise County as lawmen.

15. For a discussion of *Forty Guns* in relation to genre, see Lisa Dombrowski's *The Films of Sam Fuller: if you die, I'll kill you!* (2008: 107–116).

16. For a brief discussion of Barbara Stanwyck in relation to the portrayal of powerful woman on screen that raises as many questions as it answers, see Mainon and Ursini's *Modern Amazons:Warrior Women on Screen* (2006: 328–330).

17. A discussion of *Once Upon a Time in the West* such as that of Christopher Frayling in his *Spaghetti Westerns: Cowboys and Europeans from Karl May to Sergio Leone* (1981) – see the examination of the 'train' and 'railroad,' for example, pp. 195–196 – depends on semiotic analysis, that is, on the ways in which images such as 'train' and 'railroad' can be seen to operate as signs.

18. Wyatt Earp was strongly linked to this use of the gun. One of the events that preceded the historical 'Gunfight at the OK Corral' in Tombstone involved Earp 'pistol-whipping' Tom McLaury, one of the cowboys who died in the fight that followed.

19. For a discussion that moves toward considering *Forty Guns* as the work of an auteur, see Howard Hughes's *Stagecoach to Tombstone: the Filmgoers' Guide to the Great Westerns* (2008: 95–103).

20. "The aim was to perfectly simulate the famous 'last death-rattle' as sounded on the harmonica" (Spencer, 2008: 151).

21. Naming his hero as Joachim Murat (a general under Napoleon who eventually died, reportedly heroically and without a blindfold, before a firing squad) within minutes of the film starting, Custer says: 'And his one tactic was: ride to the sound of the guns.'

22. Such an interpretation contrasts with that found in Jacquelyn Kilpatrick's *Celluloid Indians: Native Americans and Film* (1999: 52–53): 'The story was an old one that every child had learned at school – the brave General Custer and his gallant men of the Seventh Cavalry were doing their duty, making America safe for white farmers and their families, when the dastardly Sioux ambushed them and murdered every man.'

23. This, of course, needs to be seen against the agreed backdrop that up until at least the 1960s (and arguably much later): 'The vast majority of American films produced since the beginnings of cinema reflected the ethnic hierarchies of the American hegemonic order; the default ethnicity was WASP: white, Anglo-Saxon, Protestant' (Pearson and Simpson, 2001: 159).

24. See, for example, the earlier section, Silent 'Westerns,' pp. 10–16.

25. Here we are moving beyond the area of representation, in a sense, to consider ways in which acting performance might be able not only to reinforce dominant meanings but to question those very same in-place, mainstream meanings.

26. Captain Richard H. Pratt opened one of the first such boarding schools in 1879:

> His philosophy was to 'elevate' American Indians to white standards through a process of forced acculturation that stripped them of their language, culture, and customs (Smith, 2007).

27. In *Dissenting Voices in America's Rise to Power*, David Mayers lists a series of Army officers who registered their sympathy for the plight of a range of Native

American tribes in the post–Civil War period (2007: 159–189). He quotes Colonel John Gibbon of the 7th Infantry: 'How would we feel, how would we act if our country were over-run and wrested from us by another race' (p. 171).

28. Particularly as a result of the economic hardships caused for ordinary people by the Depression of the 1930s, many of those working in Hollywood had been attracted to left-wing views, and some had joined the American Communist Party. With the Cold War developing after the Second World War, the House Un-American Activities Committee (HUAC) began investigating 'subversives.' HUAC hearings in 1947 attempted to prove that Hollywood films had been used to put forward communist ideas. Some Hollywood filmmakers, mainly screenwriters, were blacklisted so that they were unable to find work in the film industry. With hysteria about communists within America increasing, the hearings were resumed in 1951. Some of those called to appear before the committee saved themselves by naming others who had been involved with left-wing activities. Some who refused to cooperate found their names added to the 'blacklist.' Foreman himself, a former member of the Communist Party, was called to testify during the filming of High Noon and later moved to England where he stayed until 1975. (See Brenda Murphy's *Congressional Theatre: Dramatizing McCarthyism on Stage, Film and Television*, 2003: 255–256).

29. Howard Hawks claimed he had made *Rio Bravo* (1959, Warners) to repudiate the view of the world put forward in *High Noon* in which the sheriff shows fear, uncertainty, and despair before finally facing up to the forces of evil on his own. By displaying confident leadership, the sheriff in *Rio Bravo*, John T. Chance (John Wayne), creates a situation in which others are able to prove their worth.

30. For details of the production of *The Alamo*, see Roberts and Olson's *John Wayne: American* (1997: 455–479).

31. 'Any discussion of *The Alamo*…cannot ignore its twin formative elements: Wayne's politics and the sociopolitical moment from which it emerges' (Flores, 2002: 114).

32. In 1824, with increasing numbers of American settlers in Texas having slaves, Mexico confirmed the abolition of slavery in its territories in a new constitution but, in Texas, slavery was simply renamed 'contract labour,' allowing workers to be held in bondage for 99 years.

33. Wayne has been quoted as saying he only ever played himself on screen, and this is very evident in this film wherein he often seems to address the audience almost as he might for a pre-election political TV address. Later, notice we do not see the death of Crockett/Wayne, which happens off-screen.

34. And, maybe not such an 'odd mixture': Gerald F. Linderman records how Wayne's macho stance had him booed off stage at a naval hospital in Hawaii in World War Two by those who knew 'the reality of combat' (1999: 316–317).

35. The theory was developed at the Centre for Contemporary Cultural Studies in Birmingham, U. K. in the 1970s (see Hall in Durham and Kellner, 2006: 163–173).

36. Though at least the key personnel of Foreman and Wayne look as if they were, at least to a large extent, aware of what was being embedded in *High Noon* and *The Alamo*.

37. Note that this may not be the same as the *intended* meaning of the encoders as encoding involves unconscious and conscious decisions.

38. Foucault (1926–84) was a French thinker concerned with the role of hegemonic power within society. His approach was essentially developed out of the Italian, Antonio Gramsci's concept of hegemony. The idea here was that an alliance, or 'historic bloc,' of social groups could achieve consent for its domination of society by controlling channels of communication such as education, publishing, and the media. This hegemony was seen as subject to continual ongoing renegotiation and redefinition. Foucault attempted to delve beneath the layer of consent to investigate how this system operated to legitimize certain expressions of power. For a short overview of discourse analysis, see Pearson and Simpson's *Critical Dictionary of Film and Television Theory* (2001: 137–139). For detail see, for example, Jorgensen and Phillips's *Discourse Analysis as Theory and Method* (2002).

39. According to Amy Greenberg, 'Americans have been slow to recognize that their republic is in fact an empire, and that its imperial history stretches back almost to the American Revolution' (2005: 18). This suggests, given these sorts of shots of the American flag in films, that the nationalist discourse is working in such a way as to create national pride without recognizing that the nation is in any way imperialistic.

40. No mention is made of the Battle of Washita in 1868, which was in fact a massacre rather than a battle in which Custer's 7th Cavalry killed more than 100 people in a charge through a sleeping Cheyenne village. (*Fort Apache* may expose the flaws in a glory-hunting cavalry officer such as Colonel Thursday, a man who has all the traits of Colonel George Armstrong Custer, but it also asserts the importance of such legends – to the nation –and the key role of the media in perpetuating such legends.)

41. In Studlar and Bernstein's *John Ford Made Westerns: Filming the Legend in the Sound Era* (2001: 110–111), following other critics, it is suggested there is a shift in Ford's representation of Indians after World War Two, with his films coming to recognize Native Americans in their own right and not simply as a threat to the white man.

42. See Ken Nolley's 'The Representation of Conquest: John Ford and the Hollywood Indian, 1939–1964' in Rollins and O'Connor's *Hollywood's Indians: the Portrayal of the Native American in Film* (2003), for a more in-depth exploration of this area of Ford's work.

43. When there is a dispute within the home Mrs. O'Rourke, is able to take control of not only her husband and son but of Colonel Thursday (Henry Fonda).

44. Note how Wayne takes on the additional male role of father-figure in *She Wore a Yellow Ribbon*. This aspect of gender discourse was taken up in *Fort Apache* by the negative model offered by Colonel Thursday (Henry Fonda) being set against the positive model shown by Sergeant Major Michael O'Rourke (Ward Bond).

45. 'Narrative develops on the basis of a chain of cause-and-effect. An event happens and is shown to have (likely) consequences. As experienced film-goers, we learn to expect and anticipate this chain, or at any rate to recognize the causal links when they are made' (Nelmes, 2003: 80).

46. This may not be quite as straightforward as suggested here: a basic difference between a traditional narrative and some modern uses of 'story' has been suggested by some theorists. 'In the traditional narrative of resolution, there is a sense of problem-solving, of things being worked out in some way…"What will happen?" is the basic question. In the modern plot of revelation, however, the emphasis is elsewhere; the function of the discourse is not to answer that question nor even pose it' (Chatman, 1978: 48).

47. The B-Westerns Wayne is involved in making throughout the 1930s classically withhold the anticipated coming together of hero and love interest in an embrace and passionate kiss until the last moment, just as the final credits begin to roll.

48. It could be that we are also engaged in constructing a narrative that spans the films in which we have seen our central star play the same type of role. 'From this standpoint, *The Outlaw Josey Wales* gives a biography to the Man With No Name – it gives him his reasons for violence, rather than wrapping that violence in mystery' (Beard, 2000: 74).

49. Perhaps, despite the high body count, this is as Neil Fulwood suggests in *One Hundred Violent Films That Changed Cinema*, 'a western about peace and unity, a western that rejects the gun' (2003: 13).

50. For a full discussion of 'realism,' the implications of the term and its use in film see Hallam and Marshment's *Realism and Popular Cinema* (2000).

51. See, for example, the vague use of the term in Buck Rainey's 'The "Reel" Cowboy' in Harris and Rainey's *The Cowboy: Six-Shooters, Songs and Sex*. 'Many pre-1920 Western films stressed realism – in fact, most' (2002: 26).

52. To use a further term, for Paul Seydor 'for all the realism of the trappings' the end result in Peckinpah's film can be an effect of 'pure myth' (1999: 353).

53. Naturalism would claim to record the closely observed detail of human life. The suggestion is that through close observation and realistic recording of human interaction, it is possible to gain a better understanding of the complexities of both individual characters and the wider society. Naturalism began as a late-nineteenth-century movement in theatre and the novel but has had an influence on film; acting, for example, has often be judged by its ability reproduce the fine detail of human behavior.

54. Expressionism uses nonrealist, abstract, angular shapes and forms, and dark shadowy lighting to convey a sense of a state of mind, often of psychological

anguish. In film, German Expressionism in the post–First World War period is seen as the forerunner of Second World War and post–Second World War film noir in America.

55. 'Not only does Sparks's presence remind the viewers that most lynching victims were African American, but he acts as the moral and spiritual conscience of the film,' (Wood 2009: 243).

56. Could it be that Tetley stands for the South as a whole and that his son's words are a condemnation of all those who have held power in that part of the United States?

57. Dana Andrews, as Donald Martin, the leader of the three men who are killed, exhibits some defiance but is neither stoical nor heroic, being reduced first to despair and then to tears.

58. Although, Stephen Prince suggests, the complexity of Peckinpah's editing in these sequences 'takes us a long way from simple realism' (1999: 28).

59. Andrew Sarris is generally credited with promoting the auteur approach of the French critics into a theory that was to become central to film studies (2005: 99–107).

60. Laura in *Bend of the River*: 'Any man can make a mistake. He can make lots of mistakes. But when he meets a woman and falls in love with her ...'

61. Both Mann and Yordan seem to have been interested in the possibilities of transferring classical tragedy to Hollywood (Winkler, 2001: 123).

62. Stars 'are composed within the field of dominant and competing definitions of society' (Turner, 1999: 123).

63. Stars 'enact ways of making sense of the experience of being a person in a particular type of social production' (Dyer, 1986: 17).

64. By 1968, there were around 500,000 American combat troops in Vietnam and, since 1961, more than 15,000 U.S. troops had been killed and well in excess of 100,000 wounded. By 1969, President Richard Nixon had begun to announce troop withdrawals after the North Vietnamese Tet Offensive of the previous year. Wayne produced, directed, and starred in the strongly pro-war *The Green Berets* in 1968. At home, demonstrations against the war took place on many student campuses in the late 1960s, and race riots caused disturbances in more than 30 cities across the country.

65. It also makes him the perfect fit for the self-image frequently carried into American foreign policy by politicians in subsequent years.

66. '...the entire logic of the story, and the genre, is rejected to accommodate the happy ending' (Grant, 2007: 70).

67. The threat (expressed in cold, measured tones just over halfway through the film) is made all the more terrifying for the audience by the knowledge that one of the key features of Wayne's star image was that this was a man who, if he made a statement, always followed through.

68. See Deborah Thomas's 'John Wayne's Body' in Cameron and Pye (1996).

69. See, for example, his *Playboy* interview (Lewis, 1971: 77).

70. For a powerfully expressed exploration of this point of view, see Yardena Rand's *Wild Open Spaces: Why We Love Westerns* (2005).

71. For a discussion of Lacan in relation to film theory, see McGowan and Kunkle's *Lacan and Contemporary Film* (2004: xi–xxix).

72. How this might be interpreted in relation to male and female spectators might be complex, especially as, in his performance, Mitchum displays a definite sense of male strength but allied to clear vulnerability. His strength is in facing his fate but not in fulfilling the male hero's more usual role of taking charge of his fate. This, incidentally, moves the film toward a classical concept of tragedy.

73. For an exploration of both of these films in relation to the darkness of film noir, see Wheeler Winston Dixon's *American Cinema of the 1940s: Themes and Variations* (2006: 195–199).

74. Mrs. McCanles tells Pearl almost as soon as she arrives: 'All you have to do is to behave like a lady.'

75. Both Jesse and Helen are highly controlled, or repressed. Cotton plays Jesse as someone continually reining in his desire for Pearl. Helen is always dressed in a very proper, covered manner (in direct contrast to Pearl's use of dress as a further means of sexual expression).

76. Lewt's 'you never rode bareback before in your life' when she falls from the horse on her first attempt fully expresses his realization that she is a virgin.

77. For an exploration of Pearl in relation to both Lewt and Jesse and an investigation of Pearl in relation to the position of the female spectator, see Laura Mulvey's 'Afterthoughts on "Visual Pleasure and Narrative Cinema" Inspired by *Duel in the Sun* (King Vidor, 1946)' (in Simpson, Utterson, and Shepherdson 2004: 68–77).

78. We can certainly be critical of this as a theoretical position, but the suggestiveness of the ideas remains strong.

> Even when Freud himself is seen as participating in a historically confined sexism in his psychic placement of women as men without penises, his ideas about the constructed nature of gender identity and the multiple identification with, and desires for, the multiple positions of the Oedipal situation have created waves in many areas of literary and cultural criticism (Thurschwell, 2000: 129).

79. As a form of incest, this parallels Adam's (John Rodney) love for his sister and completes a sibling love triangle.

80. 'I tried to figure out what crazy game you were playin' with me but I couldn't. But I knew I'd play it out with you right to the end' (Jeb).

81. *Modernity* is the term used to refer to the period of Western social development associated with industrialization and the growing urbanization of populations. Jean-Francois Lyotard (1984) describes a shift to a post-industrial economic period based on consumption, information, and the service sector and linked to the development of a global social sphere and new communications technologies.

82. 'The action of the western takes place against a backdrop of majestic landscapes that illustrates the magnitude of the principles involved and

pitted against one another in the plot and via characters: good versus evil, law and justice versus lawlessness, order versus anarchy. These principles, of course, are projections of the cultural codes or metanarratives ruling contemporary society. The typical strategy of the postmodern western is to reveal the constructed character of these principles by first invoking and then negating the conventions that embody them .'(D'haen, 1997: 186)

83. Later (having given up his bed for the American President) he says, crystallizing the false romantic note of the myth of the Frontier, 'I'll sleep out on the prairie under the moon and listen to the lullaby of the coyote before actually ending up in the bar.

84. In '"The Grandest and Most Cosmopolitan Object Teacher": *Buffalo Bill's Wild West* and the Politics of American Identity, 1883–1899,' Jonathan D. Martin says, 'Mapping out the past, the present, and the future of the United States, the show functioned as a symbolic universe that gave meaning and significance to a whole body of ideas about race, progress, civilization, and American identity' (1996: 96).

85. Of course, it may be argued that comedic works in the lineage of the Marx Brothers have always demanded just such a joyful understanding of the 'constructedness' of film.

86. Within the concept of postmodernity, the mass media that increasingly impregnate our everyday lives is seen as coming to constitute all that we know and can know. Baudrillard (1983) talks about the media as creating a blizzard of signs, an infinite unending flow of images and sounds, or a constant simulation in which we are unavoidably immersed. In this interpretation, there is no social reality that is distinguishable from the constructed media representation or simulation. The media (Baudrillard was talking in particular about TV) and the daily experience of life dissolve into one, creating a 'hyper-reality,' and we are left with a culture that is not only superficial but essentially meaningless. Maybe we wouldn't go this far; but equally, maybe this is not so far from the unending storytelling of *Buffalo Bill* and the flow of images through time and space that is created in *Blazing Saddles*.

87. 'United Artists' decision to pull *Heaven's Gate* immediately after its release has … become a kind of metaphor for what is wrong with the movie business these days,' (Egan, 1980: 16).

88. Bosley Crowther, for example, *New York Times*, May 28, 1954, condemned it as 'a flat walk-through – or occasional ride-through – of western clichés.'

89. Though recognizing the importance of the concept of audience response, an analysis such as this needs to be treated with caution and seen as an ongoing debate as, according to some ethnographic studies, the wide range of readings that actually emerge when research is conducted using focus groups resists any simple categorization. Responses do not, it seems, for example, slot easily into categories such as those posited by a theorist such as Stuart Hall of preferred, negotiated, and oppositional readings.

90. See Jim's use of a Roman tactical ploy in the final battle with the cattlemen.

91. Jim tells Canton he would need to die and be reborn to be in his class, which may conceivably cast Jim as a Christ-like figure! He is certainly

god-like in his ability to walk away from any situation, especially the final apocalyptic battle, without a scratch. It may also be the case that there is a parody at work in the way that he comes down among the people before finally ascending to his previous elevated status.

92. The cavalry officer, Frank, sees through 'Jim,' telling him: 'You're a rich man with a good name: you only pretend to be poor … You can't force salvation on people: it doesn't work.'

93. This was filmed at Oxford, perhaps indicating the significance for European and American society that Cimino saw in his film.

94. The historical picture of migrations into the West is complex, but one thing is clear according to Margaret Walsh: 'Gone is the traditional Turnerian hypothesis of a frontier melting pot with its easy rural assimilation process' (2005: 68).

95. 'In *Heaven's Gate*, Cimino makes explicit what had been merely implied in his earlier films. If his earlier films had shown the effects of the oppression and exploitation of the American working class, here he shows the concrete, violent manifestations of that oppression precisely where we least expect it – not in the teeming slums of the East, but in the wide open spaces of the West – and against rather unlikely victims – not Southern Europeans, Chinese, Indians, or Blacks, but Germanic and Slavic Europeans' (Lawton, 1994: 405).

96. 'By the early 1880s, the Northern Pacific, Santa Fe, and other transcontinental railroads possessing enormous tracts of land that they wished to convert into cash were running trains with as many as 50 cars filled with immigrants and their baggage, all from the same locality and all traveling to the same destination.' (Brown, 1978: 237)

97. 'The numerous delays and charges of reckless budgetary abuses have obscured the basic proposition the film confronts: a re-examination and an ensuing reconstruction of the mythology – social, political, and cultural – of the western as an archetype of the American experience…' (Sultanik, 1986: 348).

98. Vienna is (like the immigrants in *Heaven's Gate*) challenging the right of the wealthy cattle ranchers to own everything in the territory.

99. For Ella (Isabelle Huppert), like Vienna, economic independence is closely linked to sexual autonomy. Both know, as Vienna says, that in this male-dominated society, 'All a woman has to do is slip once and she's a tramp,' and both respond to the challenge of this in their own way.

100. Robert Schultz attempts to reassert the importance of the 'social terrain' of the film alongside the 'psychological terrain,' viewing the social order in the film as 'composed of corrupt individuals seeking their liberal self-interests' (1990: 59).

4

KEY WESTERNS

This chapter focuses on eight case studies. Several of the films under consideration are generally seen as seminal works in the history of the Western. The main effort here, though, is to further reinforce the idea of the potential offered by theoretical approaches detailed in Chapter 3. In each case, a combination of theoretical approaches is used. Close analysis of specific shots and scenes from the chosen films is included.

STAGECOACH

(1939, United Artists/Walter Wanger Productions) Director: John Ford. Screenwriter: Dudley Nichols. Cinematographer: Bert Glennan. Editors: Dorothy Spencer and Walter Reynolds. Music: Richard Hageman. Cast: John Wayne (Ringo Kid), Claire Trevor (Dallas), Thomas Mitchell ('Doc' Boone), John Carradine (Hatfield), Louise Platt (Lucy Mallory), Andy Devine (Buck), George Bancroft (Curley), Berton Churchill (Gatewood), Donald Meek (Peacock), Tom Tyler (Luke Plummer).

In this film, Ford[1] combines what in the 1930s have become effectively distinct, compartmentalized genres, A-Westerns and B-Westerns, and creates the basis for the classic Westerns of the 1940s and 1950s. The use of distinctive locations to give a sense of the huge interior of the country that is found in a film such as *The Big Trail* (1930) is adhered to but is made more manageable in budgetary terms and given greater coherence of imagery by focusing on a single grand-scale location, Monument Valley in Utah. The use of this space was to become an element of Ford's auteur signature,[2] but it had not previously been seen in films and at the time startled audiences. There are moments when the stagecoach of the title is shown being swallowed into the immensity of the desert, an image that effectively expresses the feeling of moving into the West recorded by early pioneers and travelers. The buttes that rise with sheer cliff faces out of the desert are at once both magnificent in their beauty and threatening in their towering size. Like a series of nineteenth-century American painters who represented in their work the expansion of the country into the West, however, Ford also emphasizes within this expanse the heroic stature of the individual. The first shot of the hero, the Ringo Kid (John Wayne), moves from a long shot of the character with his rifle to zoom into a close-up of his face. As in a Frederic Remington painting, the surrounding landscape falls away, and the figure takes on a monumental aspect every bit as impressive as anything Monument Valley can offer. Ford uses the camera to replicate and enhance the action of the eye drawn to the body and then the face of the figure in these paintings. Later, there is similar shot of 'the heroic individual' as a cavalry officer turning in his saddle to wave goodbye to the stagecoach fills the screen. There is not the same camera movement as in the shot of Wayne, but the angle of shot and the way it is momentarily held means we have to look up to the figure.

The dramatic action of the B-Western is provided by a chase sequence in which the stagecoach is pursued across salt flats by Apaches. Legendary stuntman Yakima Canutt, five times world champion rodeo rider and an actor in a series of B-Westerns with Wayne, is employed by Ford. The high point of a series of stunts has Canutt falling beneath the horses (and then the following wheels) of the stagecoach. *The Sagebush Trail* (1933), a B-Western, has Wayne firing from atop a stagecoach exactly as he does in this film.[3] However, Ford takes the commonplace of the B-Western and intensifies the action through his particular use of editing and camerawork. The sequence,

Figure 4.1   Heroic stature (*Stagecoach*, 1939)

for example, opens with a startling extreme close-up for the audience as Peacock (Donald Meek) falls toward the camera in the stagecoach with an arrow in his chest. The screen is filled with the arrow and Doc Boone's hand (Thomas Mitchell) grasping it to pull it out. Further into the piece, there are ground-level shots of horses being ridden toward and then straight over the camera. And between the action shots and the stunts, there is time for the drama between the inhabitants within the stagecoach to continue to unfold. An extreme close-up of Hatfield's gun (John Carradine) shows him preparing the last bullet for Mrs. Mallory (Louise Platt) before a close-up shows the gun appearing next to her head.

The 'baddies' in B-Westerns classically wear black hats, as does Canutt when playing 'Curley Joe' in *Paradise Canyon* (1935) and, in the shoot-out, the protagonists walk toward each other down the town's main street as Wayne as Singin' Sandy Saunders prepares to meet Slippery Morgan in *Riders of Destiny* (1933). Ford has Luke Plummer (Tom Tyler) wear the required hat and walk down the street with his brothers toward the Ringo Kid, but he energizes the formula through a series of innovations. Through careful direction of performance and camerawork within a few minutes of screen time, Plummer becomes a rounded character. When he stands, lighting casts the whole of Plummer's face and shoulders into shadow. When he throws his hand of cards on the table, a close-up shows us the ace of spades. When he moves to the bar, everyone else in the saloon edges away. When he takes a drink, he spills some. As he swallows, we see the movement of his throat in close-up and simultaneously the narrowing of the eyes as he looks around slowly. As all of this action involving Plummer builds toward the climactic shoot-out, it is inter-cut with shots of the drama surrounding the Ringo Kid. He is shown moving deeper and deeper into the shadowy underworld of doorway liaisons and parties in brothels that is the domain of Dallas. And when the moment of the shooting does actually begin, Ford constructs the film so that we don't see it. We hear the shots and watch Dallas as she reacts to the noises off-screen, denied a view of the action and forced like her to await the outcome. This is the classic shoot-out in a Western town that was so much a part of the genre, but it is brought to the viewer in an entirely new way. Ford doesn't stop here: when Plummer walks back into the saloon, the director's exploitation of audience expectation and his use of the twin possibilities of suspense and surprise continue as it appears Plummer is alive and, therefore, victorious.

As the shadowy final shoot-out of *Stagecoach* suggests, the Old West (and by implication, perhaps, the modern 1939-world) is a dark place but still a place within which we can imagine good triumphing, even if justice can be achieved only by a man taking the law into his own hands before fleeing across the border to another country, where it is still possible to live the 'American' Dream. In these terms, the film is incredible for the issues it fails to confront as much as for the ones it does.[4] The conservative forces of America (the righteous ladies of the Law and Order League) are ridiculed for their failure to recognize the real qualities of 'Doc' and Dallas; the snobbery of Mrs. Mallory is challenged; the old values of the South, embodied in Hatfield, are shown to be out of time and place; and those who, like Gatewood, are driven by greed and status are exposed as hypocrites. However, the rule of law doesn't function in this place, justice can be achieved only by the single strong male operating as a vigilante, and for the most honest and open male and female characters, Ringo and Dallas, there is no place in America. In thematic terms, there is hope in their union and, in narrative terms, comfort, but Lordsburg will remain a dark, noirish space and the opening town of Tonto a place of social prejudice.[5]

For a director noted for his use of the imposing Monument Valley landscape, it is claustrophobic, enclosed spaces that noticeably dominate this film.[6] Within the cramped arena of the stagecoach and low-ceilinged rooms of staging posts along the journey, the prejudices of the various characters rub against one another, the values and morals of contemporary America are questioned, and all this is set against the backdrop of the innocent (but maybe knowing) non-judgmental strength of the hero. When they reach the first stop on their journey, for example, Dallas knows her place is not at the table with the rest of American society and sits near the door. Ringo, by contrast, not only moves confidently to the table himself but then invites Dallas (addressing her respectfully as 'ma'am') into the gathered community.[7] In the coach, Ringo symbolically sits on the floor between the other characters and treats them all as equals. He joins them together at every opportunity and comments tellingly but without animosity on the actions of others. At his instigation, Hatfield does pass the canteen to the other 'lady' in the carriage, Dallas, but puts away the cup he has used in giving water to Mrs. Mallory, and Ringo's simple 'No silver cup, I guess,' with a smile to Dallas, says all that needs to be said about prejudice and hypocrisy and a lack of real Christian values.[8] Twice in the confined space of a room, Curley calls on democratic American values. In the first instance, when they have to decide whether to continue their journey without a cavalry escort, he says: 'I'll tell you how we'll settle it: we'll take a vote.' Ironically, we are then presented with a highly divided society that is unable even to sit around the same table together. Later, when they are again unsure whether to go on or not, he says: 'Let's all sit down and talk sensible.' However, again democratic principles come to nothing because, with an impending Indian attack, the time for talk has gone, and the time for action has arrived.[9]

As with a B-Western such as *West of the Divide* (1933), Ford has his central character (played by Wayne as in the B-Western) reclaiming a family for himself after his father has been killed. In both films, Wayne's character seems not only to be without a father but motherless, and in both we might see the acquired wife not only as a potential mother to this character's children but as in some sense a mother to him. In both films, Wayne plays a driven character who has to avenge the death of a father. In both, further complexity is added, in that he has something of the father about him as well (see the way he looks toward Dallas when she emerges with Mrs. Mallory's newborn child, for instance). However, where *West of the Divide* provides Wayne's character with the melodramatic possibilities of a lost and refound younger brother, Ford allows much of this to play beneath the surface of his film realizing that the potency of the implied and suggested can be greater than that which is made explicit. He explores the psychological territory of the B-Western in more subtle ways and, at the same time, places all of this within the context of wider social concerns.

This film is necessarily of its time: Native Americans are seen as nothing more than an enemy always likely to take to the 'warpath,' and older women are painted as stereotypically shrewish, for example. Yet, in the way that it cherry-picks from the available 1930s models of the Western, combining aspects of B-Westerns and A-Westerns to create a troubled complex shaping of the genre for the coming decades, this film represents a turning point. In their individual characters and in their relationship, Ringo and Dallas challenge the hypocritical notions of social rank portrayed by others, and yet, in the walk toward the final shoot-out, troubling aspects clearly attach to both. Ringo clicks the bullets into his rifle in the confident knowing manner of a man who has done all this before. Heavy shadows cross both their faces but especially Ringo's. At times, indeed, his entire body is in darkness.

MY DARLING CLEMENTINE

(1946, 20th Century Fox) Director: John Ford. Screenwriter: Samuel G. Engel and Winston Miller. Cinematographer: Joe McDonald. Editor: Dorothy Spencer. Music: Cyril M. Mockridge. Cast: Henry Fonda (Wyatt Earp), Victor Mature ('Doc' Holliday), Linda Darnell (Chihuahua), Walter Brennan (Old Man Clanton), Tim Holt (Virgil Earp), Cathy Downs (Clementine Carter), Ward Bond (Morgan Earp), Alan Mowbray (Granville Thorndyke), John Ireland (Billy Clanton).

Stagecoach was made when Ford was in his mid-forties. *My Darling Clementine* was released after the war when he is into his fifties. By this time, he has been directing films, including Westerns, for almost 30 years. In the silent period, he made a series of staple Westerns and the more usually mentioned epic, *The Iron Horse* (1924); but, although he directed two or three films a year throughout the 1930s, he only really returned to Westerns with *Stagecoach*. During the postwar period, he made a series of what are commonly recognized as classic Westerns so that this became the genre with which his name is now most closely associated. However, the connection was really established quite late in his career. For 30 years after the Second World War, the Western became not only the chief means of exploring the American past and the establishing beliefs of the United States but the key means of examining the country's role in the contemporary world. The opening 20 years of this period coincided with the high point of Ford's filmmaking.

Following on from *Stagecoach*, *My Darling Clementine* sets the parameters of style and content for everything that is to follow in Ford's postwar contributions to the Western genre. Monument Valley becomes established as the scenic backdrop.[10] This is a landscape that offers the massive scale of buttes that can seem threatening and overpowering but places these possibilities within the vast expanses of a limitless landscape stretching to distant horizons. This is a space within which human beings can quickly become small and insignificant but is also an immensity that has (in Ford's view) been, if not fully conquered, at least effectively traversed and subjected to 'progress' by the emerging United States. As the Earp brothers drive their cattle across the plains, as a stagecoach journeys between Wells Fargo staging posts or arrives at Tombstone, as Wyatt Earp (Henry Fonda) races across desert terrain in a visual reference to the short-lived period of the Pony Express riders, and as Wyatt edges his way between pioneer-style wagons in the run-up to the final shoot-out, all of these connotations (and more) that attach to the chosen location are at play. As a result, a depth of psychological implication, historical reality, and frontier myth-making are at play whenever this landscape is employed, not least in the final shot of Wyatt's riding off into that space.

In his chosen interiors, Ford flattens or adds depth to the space according to the emotional and psychological dimensions of relationships that are at play within that arena. In other words, as with outside locations, he uses his sets to enhance the drama. Depth of space is particularly used within the saloon, for example, when 'Doc' Holliday (Victor Mature) is viewed walking the full length of the bar toward a gambler he wants to 'run out of town' or when the same character, having operated on Chihuahua (Linda Darnell), is watched again walking the full length of the bar but away from the camera to leave the saloon. These moments have vastly different emotional import for the spectator, but both use depth of space as one device to express the drama. By contrast, when Chihuahua confesses to Wyatt and Doc, a series of shot configurations are used that flatten any depth and convey the claustrophobic intensity of this climactic moment in the relationship between the three characters, with the two men literally boxing her in on the screen.

Shadows, particularly across faces, are used by Ford in a variety of ways and, as the film progresses, the use of noir lighting increases.[11] As the three brothers ride out to where they have left their younger brother looking after their cattle, not only the torrential rain but the heavy shadows are full of foreboding. When Doc tells Clementine to leave Tombstone on the morning stage, he has become little more than a stark silhouette and, as immediately afterward, he retreats into his room, he loses himself (and we lose him) in the shadows, before he again becomes a silhouette, a dark, one-dimensional representation of himself. Later, when he looks down at Chihuahua after having operated on her, his face is lit from one side only[12] so that almost all of his face is cast into heavy, unnatural shadow. For his part, Wyatt on several occasions walks away from the camera and disappears into darkness. At other times, he is shown sitting on a chair on the boardwalk in what becomes a character-defining position, rocking backward and forward on the border between the shadows and sunlight.

The composition of certain shots, combined with the way in which Ford momentarily holds these shots as if to allow the viewer to absorb the image, means individual framings 'live' beyond the end of the film. The face of the youngest brother, James Earp (Don Garner), lit in close-up for the viewer to register his youth and note his admiration for his brothers as they ride off into town ... James lying dead in the mud in the foreground of a shot, his body creating a strong horizontal line across the frame, his leg twisted up awkwardly still in the stirrup of his riderless horse, which stands behind him ... Wyatt in the bottom right-hand corner of the frame riding away from James's grave, which is placed in the centre of the screen with a cleft butte of Monument Valley in the distance: these are three

Figure 4.2   Dead in the mud (*My Darling Clementine*, 1946)

shots that, like a triptych, encapsulate the youth, death, and afterlife of an innocent. In the second of these shots, what we have is James prone when he should be standing, still when he should be animated, accompanied by the horse he won't be riding into the future. What exists on the screen exists in relation to a series of other possibilities and, by fractionally holding shots, Ford not only grants us the time to consider these sorts of mental extensions of the image but insists we take the 'painting' with us for future reference.

There are no words in these sorts of shots; the image speaks for itself. Indeed, the paring back of dialogue is in itself a feature of Ford's work. The sequence in which the older Earp brothers find their younger brother's body is almost entirely silent. One of them says, 'The cattle's gone' and, as an audience, we are left with this concept of something being missing as we are shown the wagon and the area around it where we have last seen James standing and then close-ups of the pots and pans that from the earlier scene we associate with James. The only other word comes as Wyatt calls his young brother's name. Later, there is another example of this sparing use of dialogue as Wyatt and Clementine (Cathy Downs) are shown watching the dancing. They stand next to each other in a two-shot. No words are exchanged, but as we cut back and forth between them and the dancing, their performances register the fact that they both wish to join in. At another point, this time at the end of the film after the final shoot-out, Morgan (Ward Bond) has to tell Wyatt that Doc has been killed but, again, this is achieved through looks and intonation in the delivery of the minimal words that are used. The only dialogue is:

Morgan: Wyatt.
Wyatt: Doc?
Morgan: Yeh.[13]

This taut, spare use of language seems at odds with the space given to an actor to declaim Hamlet's famous soliloquy. Although the speech is broken up in a series of ways that heightens the immediate drama in the saloon and further develops both Doc's character and his relationship to Wyatt, we are in fact presented with almost the entire 'To be, or not to be...' soliloquy from Act 3, Scene 1 of Shakespeare's play. This is a stunning sleight-of-hand by Ford, a third of the way through a Western. The actor Granville Thorndyke (Alan Mowbray) brings comic relief to the film but, like a fool in a Shakespearean tragedy, the words he is given carry us to the very heart of the matter. Within the structure of the film, he is an aside who in strict adherence to Hollywood standards could be cut away because he fails to move the narrative action forward. However, what he does do is to draw attention to the inaction at the centre of Ford's film, the inaction of Wyatt. His youngest brother has been killed, he muses beside the grave about a time when 'kids like you will be able to grow up and live safe,' there's little doubt the Clantons are responsible, and yet he does nothing. He has the power: he needs only a hand-size rock to deal with the drunk, 'Indian Charlie,' who terrifies the rest of the town; he subdues the four Clanton brothers on his own, pistol-whipping one and shooting the gun from the hand of another; he allows Doc to draw first in their shoot-out but still wins comfortably, again shooting the gun from his opponent's hand. He sends a second brother, Virgil (Tim Holt), to his death in pursuit of Billy Clanton (John Ireland) with a simple, 'Go get him, Virg,' seemingly then forgetting about him until his body is dumped in the street by the Clantons. The final words of Hamlet's speech (the ones we don't get to hear because of Doc's coughing fit) are directly applicable to Wyatt:

And thus the native hue of resolution
Is sicklied o'er with the pale cast of thought,
And enterprises of great pitch and moment
With this regard their currents turn awry
And lose the name of action.

Although the scene that features the rest of this soliloquy seems to be about Doc contemplating his own death, it is more profoundly related to Wyatt.[14] And what is his role throughout this scene: he is, as he often is, the observer. In the film, he continually watches and waits, rocking himself on his chair between light and dark, trying to find the point of balance between the two, playing his role as if he is playing a hand of poker.[15] At the heart of this film, and at the heart of Ford's auteur signature, is always a central character who is an enigma. Every other aspect of his approach toward film construction serves the purpose of deepening the mystery around this character. The ending leaves the audience with only further uncertainties, and the final kiss is awkward, frustrating, and full of further prevarication.

All of this makes for interesting texts that explore the complexity of human nature and relationships, but it does ignore the extent to which Ford is involved in constructing myths not only about the Old West but about the United States as a nation. 'Indian Charlie' is literally the butt of a joke as he is kicked out of town by Wyatt. Addressed not by name but as 'Indian,' he becomes all Native Americans as he is told to 'get outta town and stay out,' banished beyond the bounds of civilized society. Chihuahua seems more likely to be Mexican but is threatened by Wyatt with being run out of town 'back to the Apache reservation where you belong.' All ethnic minorities, it seems, can be lumped together and dealt with in the same manner. When the Clantons are forcing Thorndyke to recite to them, Ford incorporates a shot of a crowd of Mexicans in the saloon, thereby associating them with the brutal, bullying brothers. However, when Doc enters, he moves the Mexicans out of his way with a simple brush of his hand and without even looking at them. It is true that for the drama of the situation, the intensity of his gaze has to be on the actor proclaiming the lines from 'Hamlet,' but the casual dismissal of the hand gesture remains. Ford is keen to promote the concept of the move into the interior of America as the bringing of civilization. Clementine and all decent folk, Wyatt tells Doc, are welcome to stay in the town. Key social institutions are taking shape: the church may as yet be only a skeleton, but it is being built, Clementine is staying in the town to start a school, and Wyatt, of course, has brought law and order.[16] It is easy to forget that all of this amounts to the presentation of a very particular shaping of history.

SHANE

(1953, Paramount) Director: George Stevens. Screenwriter: A. B. Guthrie from novel by Jack Schaefer. Cinematographer: Loyal Griggs. Editor: William Hornbeck and Tom McAdoo. Music: Victor Young. Cast: Alan Ladd (Shane), Jean Arthur (Marian Starrett), Van Heflin (Joe Starrett), Brandon De Wilde (Joey Starrett), Jack Palance (Wilson), Ben Johnson (Chris Calloway), Emile Meyer (Rufus Ryker), Elisha Cook (Frank Torrey).

Shane has frequently been described as a 'classic' Western[17] but should more correctly be seen as a distinctively different one-off. The use of a child as a central character marks it out as something unusual within the genre. From the outset, we either see things directly from Joey's point of view or, by cutting to see his reaction, we are encouraged to consider how events are playing out from his perspective and within his child's imagination. The opening shots are of Shane (Alan Ladd) riding down into, and beginning to cross, an expansive valley with mountains in the distance, but the first character we are introduced to in close-up is Joey. Significantly, he is immediately placed in the role of observer, and the figure he is watching is the one that is going to fascinate his young mind throughout the film.[18]

Shane exists, both in the film narrative and within the audience's perception, only in relation to Joey. When the cattle baron's brother arrives at the homestead toward the end of the film to attempt to lure Joe into a trap, a change has come over Shane: he has taken out his gun. There is a noir-like shot of Shane in the window of an outhouse with the barrel of his six-gun resting on the sill, but this is only part of what we are shown: to the left of the shot just below the level of the window, Joey is standing with his back against the outhouse. Both Joey and Shane are dressed in

Figure 4.3   Joey and Shane (*Shane*, 1953)

blue shirts: younger brother and older brother, child and father-figure. The centrality of the linkage of the two within the narrative has never been clearer. The decision Shane has made is shown to us in relation to Joey and his experience of it. To make this clear, what follows is a reverse shot from inside the outhouse through the window. The darkness is even more pronounced. There are initially just three points of light: one revealing a little of Shane's face, another glinting on the barrel of his gun, and a third lighting part of Joey's face, outside looking in and level with the gun. As Joey looks up at Shane, the lighting catches the whites of his eyes.

A little later, when Joey's real father and Shane, the man he has come to idolize as a father-figure, are fighting outside their log-cabin home, the camera remains inside following Joey and his mother as they move from window to window. Effectively, as an audience, we are encouraged to experience Joey's frustration at being unable to see what is happening. When he does eventually move outside, the spectacle of the fight is shown from a small child's perspective: we are given a sense of fear as we view the action between the hooves of horses, we are given an experience of chaos through the disjointed nature of edited images, and we feel Joey's emotional disturbance reflected in the penned terror of the cattle.

Because of the process of viewing and being viewed with which the film opens, Joey and Shane are linked from the outset. If there is a bond between Shane and Marian (Jean Arthur) that, within the dominantly expressed values of the time (and within the value system of each of these characters) can never speak its name, there is by contrast a very tactile, physical relationship between Shane and Joey. Frequently, Shane stands or sits with Joey in the background of a shot, often with his arm around him. Joey is part of a close-knit family unit but, as a child, his role is to grow to be an adult and at some point leave the parental family. When Marian joins her husband, Joe Starrett (Van Heflin) in the foreground, Joey is often seen next to Shane behind them, related to them but slightly apart from them. At the Independence Day celebrations that also mark Joe and Marian's wedding anniversary, the couple link arms beneath an arch of greenery. Because of the way the shot is framed, Joey and Shane are still beneath the arch with Joe and Marion but they are set back behind them and to the right of them and therefore apart from them.

The classic love triangle that might be formed by Joe and Marian and Shane is disrupted by the presence of the child, Joey and, perhaps as a result of this, Marian often seems uncertain how to treat Shane. When the male homesteaders are having a meeting, Shane accepts his exclusion and retreats outside, literally identifying with and taking up his outsider status. Joey and his mother open the window to talk to him. At first Marian talks to him with the caressing tenderness of a lover ('I think we know ... Shane.'),[19] before suddenly changing the delivery to that of a mother addressing a child ('Shane, don't just stand there in the rain, you'll catch your death of cold'). A little later, when she is tending his cuts and bruises after he and Joe have been in a fist fight with the Riker gang, she dabs his cuts like a mother and says like a mother, 'It does smart, I know.' However, experiencing such tactile closeness to Shane has had an effect, and she has to reaffirm her marital bond ('Joe, hold me. Don't say anything, just hold me: tight.'). She is able to see her position through Joey. Her desire to stand next to Shane is no less than Joey's. She tells Joey, but is really telling herself: 'He'll be moving on one day and you'll be upset if you get to liking him too much.'

Much about this film is 'Technicolor' in its vivid and brash presentation of very obvious, stereotypical melodramatic moments and emotions. There are times such as the Independence Day scene already mentioned,

Figure 4.4   The American flag (*Shane*, 1953)

or the scene involving a wild deer coming into the Starretts' garden, or the sequence showing homesteaders riding in wagons through a verdant landscape, where the film veers toward the Western musical genre. Yet, there is also disturbing realism in a scene such as that in which one of the homesteaders, Torrey, is killed by the professional gunslinger Wilson (Jack Palance). The diminutive Torrey is made to slip and slide his way through the mud of the main street as he moves toward Wilson in a series of movements that are full of foreboding for the audience. He has been constructed within the narrative in such a way as to make it clear that he is likely to be killed at some stage. When his death arrives, he is shown being blown off his feet and backward into the mud by the force of the impact before his body is unceremoniously dragged away through the mud by another homesteader.[20]

The editing[21] provides further moments of shock. When Wilson first arrives in town, he traverses the distance from the swinging saloon doors to the bar in a dissolve that in itself displays his confident power but also serves to further emphasize his potential for violence by bringing one of his guns into sudden threatening prominence in the shot. Prior to the Independence Day celebrations, there is a highly contrived shot of the same character through a hole in the saloon door, but this is followed by a further startling edit: Wilson looks toward the camera, and his smile becomes superimposed by and then dissolves into the American flag. How are we to interpret the association of these images? Is it that gunslingers such as Wilson threaten the values embodied in the flag? Or is some more disturbing linkage, rather than opposition, implied? In the acting there are examples of real subtlety in both performance and the delivery of lines. When Joe flies at Shane and begins the fight between them, his action has been carefully motivated by the unspoken presence of Shane in his previous conversation with his wife, Marian.[22] At the moment when Shane and Marian would kiss in a less deliberately restrained film, something altogether different takes place:

> Please, Shane,...[she moves towards him]...please,...[they shake hands]...take care of yourself.

So, although it is true that we have displayed in this film a classic Western scenario of the restrained outsider hero riding into town to protect the community and taking decisive violent action only after he has tried to avoid the use of force, we also have something distinctively different in its combination of narrative, genre, and film construction. Shane is the ideal American, the strong defender of rights, never backing down from confrontations but equally never resorting to aggression until it becomes unavoidable.[23] Joe is the organizer of an emerging democracy, setting up meetings and reminding everyone that they will 'hear everybody in their turn.' The Starrett family does embody the American Dream of a loving, nurturing unit working hard but equally being provided for by a land that is bountiful. And yet, the fault-lines exposed within the family, and within the myth, although papered over in a comforting sugary coating, remain barely contained beneath the surface of the film.

THE GOOD, THE BAD, AND THE UGLY/
IL BUONO, IL BRUTTO, IL CATTIVO

(1966, Arturo Gonzalez Producciones/Constantin Film/Produzioni Europee Associati, Italy-Spain-West Germany) Director: Sergio Leone. Screenwriters: Age & Scarpelli, Sergio Leone, and Luciano Vincenzoni. Cinematographer: Tonino Delli Colli. Editor: Nino Baragli. Music: Ennio Morricone. Cast: Clint Eastwood (Blondie), Lee Van Cleef (Angel Eyes), Eli Wallach (Tuco), Aldo Giuffre (Union captain), Mario Brega (Cpl Wallace), Luigi Pistilli (Father Pablo Ramirez), Al Mulock (One-armed bounty hunter), Antonio Casas (Stevens).

Although on closer inspection Westerns always express more moral ambiguity and uncertainty about supposedly consensual values than surface readings generally allow, the heroes of these films often seem closer to superheroes in the potency with which they defend what is 'Right.' However, in the United States in the early 1960s, the comfortable and comforting victory of 'good' over 'evil' was ripe for reappraisal if Westerns were to remain marketable products. The youth culture that had emerged in the 1950s was moving into a new gear, vocal oppositional politics were being developed, and there was a growing radicalization of minority groups.[24] Furthermore, all of this was coinciding with the extension of TV ownership into almost every home and the decline of Hollywood's media dominance.

The required revisioning of the genre was initially achieved within films emerging from outside of America. Italian 'spaghetti' Westerns realized new market possibilities, reshaping the genre in such a way as to reflect contemporary (perhaps, in some senses, particularly Italian) concerns.[25] The world of the spaghetti Western was a totally male-dominated place of brutal, coldly calculated violence. Women barely figure at all in *The Good, The Bad, and the Ugly*: the first woman we see is initially simply dismissed from the presence of the men and then, when she returns to find her husband and eldest son dead, responds by fainting, and the second is dumped in the street by a wagonload of men who (it is implied) have just raped her and is then immediately beaten for information by Angel Eyes (Lee Van Cleef). This is a world in which everybody has a price on his or her head that can be collected, a world of contract killings, feuds, and revenge. It is a world in which few people have any wealth and everybody is motivated

by greed and self-preservation. Lifeless, drab towns in which the only time
the community comes together is to watch mute and impassive as another
hanging takes place are seemingly dotted across an arid, unproductive desert
landscape. In every scene, men are involved in fighting and killing or the
tracking of others to fight and kill them. Those who have been disfigured,
left scarred, or without legs or arms appear through the film. Death stalks
every character and is often outwitted only by the intervention of Fate, or
chance events. When two adversaries gain the advantage over Blondie (Clint
Eastwood) and Tuco (Eli Wallach) by coming up behind them in a shoot-
out, cannon shot from the Civil War bombardment of the town lands in the
street, creating a smokescreen and destroying their advantage.[26]

Leone's film depends for much of its success on an understanding, a
knowing relationship, existing between the filmmaker and the audience.
When Tuco and his henchmen are attempting to stalk their way toward
Blondie in his hotel room while he (initially unaware of their presence)
dismantles his gun, he lifts the pistol barrel to his eye like a telescope and, if
we know Sam Fuller's *Forty Guns* (1957), wherein we have seen this before in
a Western, we expect a circular point of view shot replicating what Blondie
can see down the barrel to follow. However, it doesn't: we have been tricked.
Our expectations have been undermined, our pleasure magnified, and our
intimacy with the director intensified.[27] Shortly afterward, Tuco tracks and
captures Blondie but, in the lead up to the capture, we are tricked several
times by Leone's direction of performance, use of editing, and employment
of off-screen space into having expectations that are immediately undercut.
The jokes, one after the other in the space of a few minutes, are on us, but
we do not feel belittled; quite the contrary, we feel elevated, particularly as
our pact with the director is sealed by a black comedy punch line at the end
of the sequence (over which we come together with the director and laugh
in unison) as 'Shorty' (a character we have never met and now never will)
is hanged.

This audience–filmmaker complicity is developed from the outset
through the way in which the first two key characters are introduced. At
the opening of the film, we are tricked into believing a gunfight is about
to erupt between two groups of cowboys entering a small, rundown town

Figure 4.5 'Nice family' (*The Good, the Bad, and the Ugly*, 1966)

from opposite ends of the mainstreet. When our expectations are pleasurably undercut, we straightaway feel ourselves to be in the hands of a director who confidently knows the genre language. The playful nature of the 'ride' we can expect is confirmed when text proclaiming Tuco to be 'the ugly' appears on-screen. However, the stakes are then increased as the serious dimension to the film is fully revealed to genre aficionados with the introduction of the second character, Angel Eyes. In just the same way that Alan Ladd as Shane comes into the film *Shane* (1953), so this character arrives out of the distance on horseback and is first seen by a young boy who runs to tell his father. However, Angel Eyes is not here to protect the family (and the associated social value system) – quite the reverse. He comments on the 'nice family' and then destroys it; leaving the boy to survey the wreckage. The initial fascination and fear shown by Joey, the boy in *Shane*, in relation to the six-gun and the man who can use it is brought into devastating relief. The boy in this film stands over the body of his older brother in the middle ground of a shot, watching his mother faint over the body of his father in the foreground, while behind him there is the empty doorway through which Angel Eyes has just passed. The extremes of calculated violence for which the film was initially criticized are brought into clear relief by this scene and by the next action of Angel Eyes, when he appears to be about to smother a man in his bed but proceeds to shoot him (four times!) in the face through the pillow, and we are left to contemplate in close-up the resulting smoke emerging from a hole in the pillow. Even here, what many spectators might notice is again the undercutting of expectations followed by a wry (black) humor.

When later the Union captain (Aldo Guiffre) calls on Blondie and Tuco (and us) to 'Come along and enjoy the spectacle' as his troops engage the Confederate forces, this is a bitterly ironic comment on war and our relationship to it, but it is also the general call Leone is making throughout this film to his audience. We are asked to 'enjoy' his knowing handling of the genre but, in keeping with the playful/serious dichotomy of his film as a whole, we are also being asked to consider the sanitized version of the West more generally brought to us by the Western. When Blondie and Tuco go to blow up the bridge between the armies, there are elements of slapstick comedy at work: the box has 'Explosives' written on it like something out of a silent comedy, and when the box gets too heavy, we hear muffled off-screen cries as our 'heroes' mug a stretcher-party and badly wounded man for the use of their stretcher! Then, just a while later the mood is entirely serious and somber as Blondie covers a young, dying man with his coat and gives him a last smoke. When Tuco finds the cemetery where the treasure is buried, the fact that it is absolutely vast is both humorous (in that he now has to find one grave among these ranks that disappear into the distance) and, like real military cemeteries across America, the ultimate comment on both the carnage and the insanity of war. It is a joke when Tuco mistakes the detachment of troops riding toward them as Southern forces only to find they are Northern soldiers with a layer of dust on their uniforms; but the serious point of the thinness of the veneer between two sides who are at war and that what they are covered in is dust (as in 'ashes to ashes, dust to dust') is also present.

Because of the playfulness, the seriousness is easy to miss but, throughout the film, Death is never far away. Men can be forced to carry their own coffin to a seemingly random spot by the side of the main street where they are summarily executed. Men will at one moment be undertaking commonplace hospitable or cleansing acts, such as eating together or taking a bath, and in the next moment they will be killing one another. In this way, killing becomes an everyday act that men undertake, a social norm.

Because of the playfulness, the main characters can be seen as merely superficial but, in fact, both in themselves and in their relationship to each other, Tuco and Blondie are used to suggest further depths of consideration for us. The link between Tuco and Blondie, for example, is that they are both 'alone.' As Tuco says at one point: 'Like me, Blondie: we are all alone in the world.' When abstracted from its context, the sense in which this could be a general comment about the human condition becomes clear. The harsh nature of Tuco's life is emphasized in the scene with his brother, Father Pablo Ramirez (Luigi Pistilli). The gulf between the two is displayed in a single shot in which Pablo's face is in close-up at the extreme right of the frame while Tuco is to the extreme left in mid-shot with his back turned toward his brother. Further, Tuco's ethnicity as Mexican and, therefore, the excluded 'Other' is emphasized at various points; for example, when he puts on the sombrero in the gunsmith's shop. This is an outsider status with which Blondie increasing identifies, not least in swapping his long coat for a poncho at the point at which he displays compassion for the dying soldier. Both Tuco and Blondie are absolutely ruthless when their liberty, their freedom to roam, is threatened: Tuco kills Wallace by repeatedly bashing his head against a rock, Blondie brutally shoots without compunction the man Angel Eyes has sent to follow him.

However, a word of caution, despite the fact that the representation of the West may have changed, despite the fact that war is questioned, despite the fact that an increasing empathy with Tuco is expressed, in the end, we conclude with the same victory of good over evil that has always been the staple of the Western: Angel Eyes is killed by Blondie.[28] Maybe all *The Good, The Bad, and The Ugly* does is to reconfigure the same moral world into a more palatable form for a new, more knowing, generation. Maybe audiences emerge(d) believing in the ultra-cool, increased cynicism of a more violent form of 'Good,' a 'Dirty Harry' style of dealing with a changing and confusing world.

The nature of the world as seen by this film is summed up in lines of dialogue that parallel one another and are given to Tuco and Blondie. At one point, Tuco tells Blondie,: 'There are two types of spurs: those that come in by the door and those that come in by the window' (i.e., there are honest, straightforward but ultimately naïve people and more-cautious, deceptive, but ultimately sensible types). Later, Blondie tells Tuco, 'You see, in this world there are two kinds of people, my friend: those with loaded guns and those who dig' (i.e., those with power and those who are powerless). However, putting power in the form of a 'loaded gun' in the hands of Blondie would seem to offer little sense of a social solution.[29]

McCABE & MRS. MILLER

(1971, David Foster Productions/Warner Brothers) Director: Robert Altman. Screenwriters: Altman and Brian McKay. Cinematographer: Vilmos Zsigmond. Production designer: Leon Ericksen. Songs by Leonard Cohen ('The Stranger Song,' 'Sisters of Mercy,' and 'Winter Lady'). Cast: John McCabe (Warren Beatty), Mrs. Miller (Julie Christie), Sheehan (Rene Auberjonois), Lawyer Clement Samuels (William Devane).

As a lone stranger rides slowly into town, the hero walks out to confront him, his coat pushed back to reveal his gun in its holster. The camera zooms in on the stranger's taut face and every element of performance and cinematography works to evoke the classic Western shoot-out. A series of recent scenes have already suggested the 'baddies' are out to gun down the central character, John McCabe, and it looks as if the moment for this to happen has arrived. However, this heavy use of genre convention is immediately and unexpectedly undercut by the simple, honest smile that comes across the face of the new guy in town, 'Cowboy' (Keith Carradine). This conveys Altman's approach to filmmaking in microcosm: let the audience think they know where the film is going and then present them with the opposite of their expectations. So, this is a Western, but it is not set in a dry, dusty, desert-like landscape. Instead, we find ourselves in a wet, heavily coniferous-forested, mountain region where, if it is not raining, it is snowing and a cold wind forms a constant whistling backdrop. Our hero is a gambler and, as such, a stereotype from previous films in the genre; he is also a 'businessman' of sorts but very definitely not the classic gunman or lawman. Our female lead, the romantic 'love-interest,' is the stereotypical 'whore-with-a-heart' but, at the same time, much more complex and enigmatic than this might suggest. We know these characters via genre convention, and yet, we do not know them in that Altman continually subverts or counterpoints the conventional character types. The same pattern is followed with plot devices;

there is a final shoot-out, for example, but it is not conducted in the open, in the more usual 'walking-toward-each-other-in-main-street' way. Instead, characters sneak around town in a lethal game of cat-and-mouse.

The film is set around 1900 in Washington State and shows the early development of a town called 'Presbyterian Church' on the back of zinc mining. Period authenticity was important for the filmmakers. Without ever seeing anything of the working conditions, it is made very clear that life in these sorts of towns was hard: disputes, arguments, and fights break out easily. The set was built in part (on a site near Vancouver, Canada) before shooting began, but then work continued during the shoot so that the film in effect showed a 'boom' town emerging and workmen constructing buildings became 'extras.' Buildings were made to be habitable and were then used as living quarters by the crew and for shooting indoor scenes. For his DVD commentary on the film, Altman describes how he wanted the clothing and the set to reflect the reality of the period. People did not, for example, he says, wear traditional Western genre 'cowboy hats' in a town such as this. A sense of the mixture of ethnic backgrounds present in such a town is given through the use of different accents, and the brutal prejudice of the divide between 'whites' and the Chinese is made abundantly clear. Butler, the main 'heavy' employed to kill McCabe when he refuses to sell his business interests to a corporation keen to 'invest' in the town, uses a cultivated English accent. He tells the men at Sheehan's bar how they could improved their productivity in the zinc mines by making better use of the Chinese:

> Up in Canada right now, they're blasting tunnels under $10 a foot, all done with 'the pigtail.' They've got some new explosives up there; fantastic stuff. You give it to Johnny Chinaman, send him in, and down comes 50 tons of rock and one dead Chinaman. Do you know what the fine is for killing a Chinaman? $50 maximum. The inspector's working for the company: four times out of five it's an accident.[30]

However, beyond the attempt to make sure that period detail is as correct as possible and to give a real sense of the harsh experience of living in a mining community around the turn of the century, such elements of film construction as the accents employed and the clothing being worn are also critical to giving a sense of character and character relationships. However, what exactly these features tell us about characters is problematic. Is Butler, for example, really from an upper-class British background, or has he simply adopted a particular way of speaking? We never know. In fact, we never know anything for certain about the pasts of any of these characters. When McCabe first enters the town, it is made clear that he is using his appearance to create a certain impression. It is freezing cold, but he takes off his buffalo-skin coat to display more clearly his suit, his black gloves, cravat, and bowler hat and, by the time he enters the bar, he has taken out a cigar. The notion of the West as a place where it is possible to escape the past and to reinvent yourself is clearly part of what we are seeing in the presentation of these characters, but so too is the idea that the 'game' of the presentation of the self to others is one in which we are all engaged on a daily basis. The crude, down-to-earth Mrs. Miller immediately sees through McCabe's presented self:

> Ya know, if you wanta make out you're such a fancy dude you oughta wear something besides that cheap Jockey Club cologne.

However, she too has several other selves: the sophisticated lady capable of wearing expensive clothes and walking with grace, the demure beauty waiting for McCabe to join her in bed, the hard-nosed businessperson cutting a deal, the tender sisterly woman looking after the vulnerable Ida. She is often referred to as 'Mrs. Miller,' but she is also called 'Connie' and (by McCabe) 'Constance.' To what extent and in what ways does her life amount to a deception, or a 'con'? To what extent are the various aspects of her life about 'conning' others? Does she have any 'constancy'? And, if so, where in her character is that 'constancy' to be found? Mystery surrounds each of the characters but perhaps particularly Mrs. Miller. How does she feel about McCabe? McCabe himself never knows, and neither do we. Her opium habit (and her range of personae) operate as an escape but might also be seen as being used as a form of protection.[31]

'Cowboy' is often seen by critics as the most vulnerable character in his open, wide-eyed, youthful innocence, but McCabe, despite his constructed air of confidence, is also presented as an innocent abroad and, in many ways, as naïve as 'Cowboy.' 'I know what I'm doing. I know what I'm doing,' he says, and it is the repetition of the phrase that indicates his doubt, his uncertainty, and his vulnerability (as well as the fact that he clearly does not know what he is doing). Several characters could be read in relation to the concept of vulnerability. Mrs. Miller refuses to show her vulnerability. Ida, a 'mail-order bride' for one of the men in the town, in her wide-eyed fearfulness, is vulnerability personified. The young person (chosen by Altman for his boyish looks) who kills 'Cowboy' is undeveloped as a character but is a frightening expression of vulnerability turned in a different direction. One of the features of the landscape chosen for the film is that it eschews the wide-open spaces often employed in the Western genre. Instead, the dark, low-ceilinged rooms and the even darker, enclosing spaces of the forest speak of entrapment. 'Cowboy' and the 'kid' who shoots him are trapped on the wooden swing bridge facing each other with their characters allowing no way out for either of them other than the inevitable outcome. McCabe in the final scenes is nervous in his movements (so much so that at certain points he becomes almost a figure of comedy). In this part of the film, he is often dwarfed by the landscape and buildings around him, small and insignificant within the frame, and frequently boxed within small rooms or within enclosed spaces within the frame.

A further possibility, thematically, would be to see the entire film in terms of an examination of power. McCabe does not just want to present himself to others in a certain way but wants to be able to see himself as somebody of status and importance. Mrs. Miller seeks to have power and control over her own life.[32] Real power clearly lies with companies such as the Harrison Shaughnessy Mining Company, which are able, through the use of wealth or force, to obtain any outcome they require. The lawyer who McCabe turns to for help is certainly seeking power, political power:

> The law is here to protect the little guy like yourself, McCabe. And, I'm
> at your service free of charge ... It would be an honour for the next

Figure 4.6 Painting with light (*McCabe and Mrs. Miller*, 1971)

senator of the state of Washington to be your servant before the scales of justice.

But, despite his grand words, the reality is somewhat different; nothing more is heard of the law and the newspapers, and McCabe is left with only his own wits for protection.

Focusing on a thematic approach to *McCabe and Mrs. Miller* would seem to ignore the immediately most striking element of the film: its cinematography. Careful use of lighting, color filters, and 'flashing' of the film[33] has given a sense of both location and period but has also created a noir-like mood of threat and foreboding. That is to say, the cinematography has reinforced and is part-and-parcel of the presentation of the thematic concerns previously identified. Altman says on the DVD commentary that he thinks of film as a painting, and this is perhaps particularly apparent in those scenes wherein small light sources are used to illuminate some areas of the screen and to cast others regions into shadow. There is a strong Irish American contingent present in Presbyterian Church, an ethnic group tragically associated in their homeland with reliance on the staple crop of potatoes, and Van Gogh's 'The Potato Eaters' (1885)[34] could have been the blueprint for much of the 'painting' with light undertaken here by Altman and and his cinematographer, Vilmos Zsigmond.

UNFORGIVEN

(1992, Malpaso Productions/Warner Brothers) Director: Clint Eastwood. Screenwriter: David Webb Peoples. Cinematographer: Jack N. Green. Editor: Joel Cox. Music: Lennie Niehaus. Cast: Clint Eastwood (William Munny), Gene Hackman (William 'Little Bill' Daggett), Morgan Freeman (Ned), Richard Harris (English Bob), Jaimz Woolvett (Schofield Kid), Saul Rubinek (W. W. Beauchamp), Frances Fisher (Strawberry Alice), Anna Thomson (Delilah), Anthony James (Skinny).

This has been described as a 'revisionist' Western, that is, one in which the myths of the Old West perpetuated and elaborated upon in Hollywood films throughout most of the twentieth century are revisited in order that a more realistic version of that period in U. S. history might emerge. The question is to what extent this is true of this film. As the star of the piece, Clint Eastwood carries with him a back catalog of roles both in Westerns and other films in which he has played cynical, hard-bitten heroes who are prepared to be absolutely brutal in delivering 'justice.'[35] If this film is to be seen as truly re-evaluating the heroic frontier myth as displayed in paintings, 'dime novels,' Wild West shows, and Hollywood films, it needs centrally to address the role of Eastwood as hero. As we have seen in *The Good, The Bad, and the Ugly*, despite critical issues being raised, this same star finally adopts the ascribed role of mythological all-American hero. First impressions might suggest a similar trajectory is followed in this film.

The first scene to focus on the central character, William Munny (Eastwood), portrays him as a poor dirt farmer in Kansas around 1880. He has a young son and daughter and is referred to as 'Pa.' The camera moves in close at ground level to show him in the mud struggling to separate healthy pigs from those with 'fever.' Interspersed high-angle shots show his hair to be grey and thinning. The family's cabin is revealed to be so small that with the front and back doors open, there is a view through to the landscape beyond.[36] The farm feels like a failing enterprise by contrast with the farmstead run by Ned Logan (Morgan Freeman) and his wife, Sally Two Trees (Cherrilene Cardinal).

When Munny arrives at Logan's[37] a little later in the film, he approaches it across a river and rides toward it through a lush, green valley.

> Americans opened up more farmland during the last third of the
> nineteenth century than during all of the nation's previous history. The
> most productive of these were the prairie lands of Minnesota, Iowa,
> and eastern Nebraska and Kansas, where adequate rainfall nourished
> tall and luxuriant grasses and loamy topsoil that was several feet deep.
> Here, settlers found it possible to transplant the 'corn and hog' farm
> economy of the Mississippi valley.
>
> (Hine and Faragher, 2007: 136)

African Americans such as Logan[38] moved into Kansas during the 1870s.
The numbers arriving steadily increased until, in 1879, there was a major
influx of more than 20,000 from the former slave states in the Southwest
(ibid: 151–152).

Farming the Plains offered a harsh, difficult existence for many settlers.
Munny's wife has died of smallpox before her thirtieth birthday around three
years before the main events of the film take place. And the final words on
the screen at the end of the film suggesting Munny eventually moved west
to California further reflect the reality for many pioneering settlers. After
several years in which the climate proved favorable for farming, droughts
from the mid-1880s through to the mid-1890s meant perhaps half the
population of western Kansas and Nebraska were forced to move out.

Before, during and after the Civil War, guerrilla bands and criminal gangs
(with the dividing line between the two uncertain) had rampaged through
states to the east of Kansas such as Missouri and Iowa. Logan and Munny
discuss the fact that it is more than 10 years since they were involved in such
violence, suggesting they were active in this way for perhaps five years after
the end of the Civil War in 1865.[39]

For a variety of reasons, the post–Civil War period is, therefore, given
a quite sound historical context. And in the first two-thirds of the film,
classic genre features that might call into question any sense of realism,
most notably the confident assurance of the hero, are consistently undercut.
Munny's son looks on in embarrassment as his father tries unsuccessfully
to mount his horse. In a scene parodying the way in which Eastwood's
character steadily regains his shooting skills in the opening to *The Outlaw*

Josey Wales, Munny is totally unable to hit a tin can with his six-gun and resorts to blasting it with a shotgun. Later, he literally and figuratively, crawls out of a saloon after being beaten by 'Little Bill' (Gene Hackman). This version of Munny reaches its zenith after this beating when, suffering from a fever, he is near to dying and sees visions of the Angel of Death with snake eyes. He cries out to Logan: 'Oh, Ned, I'm scared of dyin.' ... Oh, Ned, I'm scared. I'm tired.' The film has built toward the point where it appears we have completely lost Eastwood as the assured figure from his 'spaghetti Western' past. He has become a shadow of his former self, and it seems as if the revisionist look at the Western hero has left us with this revelation of ineptitude and all-too-human fear.

However, what then takes place is nothing less than a complete transformation as, in the final third of the film, Munny displays himself, first of all, as completely cold and calculated in killing others and then, finally, as the very embodiment of the Angel of Death in human form. From being weak and ineffective, he becomes fearfully potent and mercilessly effective. The question is: how should we read this transformation? When he leaves town at the end of the film, shots of the prostitutes might suggest they look at him in awe and admiration. The men of the town are so scared of him that they are incapable of even taking a shot at him from the shadows.

Figure 4.7   Foregrounding the rifle/gun (*Unforgiven*, 1992)

He has become the ultimate vigilante but, as such, is he presented for our admiration or revulsion? If we continue to admire him, and some audiences may chose to do so, what does it say about us and our society?

Previously, he has told Logan: 'I'm just a fella now: I ain't no different to no-one else no more,' but it seems he is different.[40] When it comes to shooting the first cowboy, there is one of several shots in the film that foreground a rifle or six-gun and have characters framed behind it. On this occasion, Logan's face is to the extreme right, and Munny is seen over the barrel of Logan's rifle. Logan cannot shoot, and Munny calmly and methodically takes over the task. After the second cowboy is killed, the Schofield Kid (Jaimz Woolvett) specifically recognizes Munny as in some way different ('I ain't like you, Will'). Munny knows exactly what the act of murder entails ('It's a hell of a thing, killing a man: you take away all he's got and all he's ever goin' t' have.') but seems able to perform it in a detached fashion. As he prepares to shoot the first young cowboy, the only concern he expresses is that he is not very good with a rifle.

It surely cannot be the case that we are supposed to revere a man who announces himself in the final shoot-out with the line: 'That's right, I killed women and children. Killed just about everything that walks or crawls at one time or another.' This is a man who, when he realizes his opponent is not dead, calmly finishes him by shooting him at point-blank range. This is the death of any semblance of the old-style Western hero (although he walks now with spurs jangling in the style of the hero of a 'spaghetti Western'). This is truly revisionist. The loss of faith is not simply in the values embodied in John Wayne in *Stagecoach* or Alan Ladd in *Shane* but in the nature of the world. Darkness has descended, and a hard rain is falling. The final sequence in the town opens with an almost pitch-black screen as Munny rides into town. Before he is finally dispatched, 'Little Bill' says, 'I don't deserve this: to die like this. I was building a house,' to which Munny replies, 'Deserve's got nothing to do with it.' We could debate whether 'Little Bill' does 'deserve' to die or not, but what Munny tells us is that 'justice' does not come into the equation, there is no such thing as 'justice.' And if this is the case, there is no such thing as 'right.' And if that is the case, there is no such thing as 'wrong.' This is so revisionist that it finally destroys the Western as a genre in the way that it has previously been configured by filmmakers and viewed by spectators.[41]

It is surely no coincidence that the writer, W. W. Beauchamp (Saul Rubinek), has written a 'dime novel' called 'The Duke of Death.' His book is supposedly about the exploits of 'English Bob' (Richard Harris), but 'The Duke' was Wayne's nickname. 'Little Bill' persistently ridicules the key character in this story as 'The Duck of Death,' perhaps reducing Wayne by a process of extrapolation to the level of a Disney cartoon character. The dangers of inflated, unrealistic stories about the West are emphasized in the romanticized understanding of gunplay displayed by the (literally) short-sighted teenager, the Schofield Kid. It may be overplayed so it becomes comic, but Munny's repeated question to Beauchamp immediately after the final shoot-out about whether he is armed is seen by the filmmakers as a serious one. What is being highlighted is the power of the 'writer' in society; the way in which false representations/lies ('There is a certain poetry to the language,' admits Beauchamp.) can have profound effects on impressionable audiences.

BROKEBACK MOUNTAIN

(2005, Alberta Film/Focus Features/Good Machine/Paramount/River Road) Director: Ang Lee. Screenwriters: Larry McMurtry and Diana Ossana. (Based on short story by Annie Proulx.) Cinematographer: Rodrigo Prieto. Editors: Geraldine Peroni and Dylan Tichenor. Music: Gustavo Santaolalla. Cast: Heath Ledger (Ennis Del Mar), Jake Gyllenhaal (Jack Twist), Anne Hathaway (Lureen Newsome), Michelle Williams (Alma), Linda Cardellini (Cassie), Anna Faris (Lashawn Malone), Randy Quaid (Joe Aguirre).

When this film was released, critics saw it as an important work that brought a challenging short story by Annie Proulx to a mainstream audience and took the Western into new territory with regard to issues of gender and sexuality. It was quickly dubbed, 'the gay cowboy movie' (Brewer, 2008: 43–45). But, is it a Western? If it is, it is projecting the usually accepted historical time frame[42] for the genre forward by 100 years to the second half of the twentieth century. However, it has already been argued in this book that having the events of *Bad Day at Black Rock* (1955) occurring in the late 1940s and setting *The Wild Bunch* (1969) just before World War One does not detract from the usefulness of reading these films as Westerns. Although there is virtually no gun-play and no clear-cut narrative clash between 'good' and 'evil' in the conventional Western sense, *Brokeback Mountain* does utilize much of the iconography of the genre, particularly in terms of dress and location. However, what really determines this film should be seen in relation to the Western is that its meanings depend upon reading it against the backdrop of the thematic concerns of that genre.[43] *Brokeback Mountain* is intimately concerned with the myth of the West, with romanticized notions of the cowboy and the pioneering life. The reality of the sudden physical violence of the historical American West has been examined by a series of revisionist Westerns stretching back to the 1960s, but this film takes a different tack, it reflects on the slow psychological violence of small-town, rural America. The dramatic landscapes of mountains and fast-flowing rivers are contrasted with the bleak monotony of the flat plain where, for example, Alma hangs out the washing. Ennis's mother and father, we might notice, have been killed when unexpectedly they have come across a bend in an otherwise completely straight road. Metaphorically, anything other than 'straight' becomes almost unimaginable within the restrictive straitjacket of this place. Paradoxically, a territory that has been lauded as a space of freedom is, in the experiencing of it, found to offer absolutely the reverse. Ennis's ever-present awareness, stemming back to the day his father has taken him as a young boy to see the dead body of a gay man, Earl, in an irrigation ditch, is that this place to which people supposedly fled to escape persecution does not tolerate difference. The dramatic battles to defend high ideals found in classic Westerns are contrasted here with the struggle to stay alive in the face of stultifying prejudices. Jack's mother embodies in her every movement and word (and, more so, in her every lack of movement, absence of words, and lack of animation) the effects of living in such a place.

Gender issues have always been at stake within the Western, so this is not essentially new territory for a 'Western' to be exploring. James Stewart challenged macho notions of the Westerner, for example, in *Destry Rides Again* (1939) and later in *The Man Who Killed Liberty Valance* (1962). Heroes such as the Ringo Kid (John Wayne) in *Stagecoach* have always been willing to extend courtesy and equality to those marked as 'outsiders' by mainstream society. Homosexual issues may always have been more submerged (or repressed), but there are clearly some very strong male bonding partnerships to be found in Westerns. Indeed, male bonding is in some respects the very essence of the genre, not only between characters within the films but between members of the audience coming together to fantasize about male prowess. Furthermore, in the emphasis given to the posturing, posing male body, there is a relationship between stars and viewers that is akin to the production and consumption of advertising. What is on sale here is male potency. Homoerotic undertones would seem unavoidable as we watch the hero (Alan Ladd) stripped to the waist (displaying his body to male, and female, members of the audience) and working with Joe Starrett (Van Heflin) to uproot a tree stump in *Shane* (1953). Even in a film as apparently violently male as *Unforgiven* (1992), what we find is an unspoken love between Eastwood as William Munny and Morgan Freeman as Ned Logan that is fully recognized by Logan's wife, Sally (Cherrilene Cardinal). What is often emphasized in the critical examination of love triangles is the struggle between two males for the love of the same woman, but this is not only to neglect but often to ignore the third side of the triangle. Sally knows that when William Munny calls for him, Ned will leave her and ride off with her 'husband.' In *The Man Who Killed Liberty Valance*, why does Donovan (John Wayne) kill Valance (Lee Marvin) for the love of Hallie (Vera Miles) or for the love of 'Rance' Stoddard (James Stewart)? These are challenging issues for Western enthusiasts, particularly for those who have invested in the Western frontier mystique of the self-contained, male loner who is able to rise, untouched, above emotional attachments. In both *Shane* and *The Man Who Shot Liberty Valance*, the male hero is shown as rising above personal love interests, putting notions of 'the family' and 'the community' above such concerns.

In the opening to *Brokeback Mountain*, Ennis Del Mar (Heath Ledger) enters a small town on his own, paralleling the oft-used format of the Western hero entering town. He leans with his back against a wall in a classic cowboy pose with his hat pulled down over his face. His movements are slow, and the pace of the editing mimics this up until the point at which there is a sudden cut to a view of Ennis from between the wheels of a passing train. The presence of the train further emphasizes the Western genre, but the violent, unexpected intrusion shocks the viewer and maybe hints at the disruption to this person's life that is shortly to occur. When Jack Twist (Jake Gyllenhaal) arrives, he immediately strikes a second classic cowboy pose, this time that of hands on hips. Both Ennis and Jack are wearing iconographic Western clothes, and some viewers might note that Jack is wearing a black hat. Ironically, these two cowboys are not employed to herd cattle but sheep.[44] However, when they are given their instructions, they are told in classic Western terms to keep their presence secretive ('No fire: don't leave no sign').

Ennis and Jake end up playing at being a 'married' couple on the mountain: while one of them goes off to work (shepherding the sheep on the high pastures), the other attends to domestic chores at the camp by the river. When Jack complains he is 'commuting' four hours a day, they switch roles. When Ennis is thrown from his horse, Jack tends his wound as a modern-relationship partner might, or maybe as an Old West 'pardner' might. Going up on to the mountain, they find themselves living in a rural idyll that, with its flowing river and background mountain scenery, resembles the Eden-like homestead of the Starretts in *Shane*. The key difference is that instead of having a solidly built log-cabin for a home like the Starretts, all Ennis and Jack have is flimsy tent. Their escape from the world cannot last, but they spend much of the rest of the film attempting to recapture the bliss of that time and place. For all the intensity of male relationships within the genre, for all the long periods spent with men and without women in reality in the early frontier days, the issue of homosexuality is not a subject usually addressed by the Western. Joe (Randy Quaid), the foreman, shows the cowboy culture's absolute rejection of gay sex ('Now, get the hell outta my trailer.'), but he also uses a descriptive phrase, to 'stem the rose,' that suggests this is not an unknown occurrence.

Ennis appears to be the classic Western hero, the loner who is self-contained and sufficient unto himself, but now he has to live with these two parts of himself. As Jack drives off after they come down from the mountain, Lee uses a classic John Ford framing device for the hero. He places Ennis in

Figure 4.8   Ennis (Heath Ledger) framed in a doorway (*Brokeback Mountain*, 2005)

a doorway but, rather than standing tall, this 'hero' is bent double, crying and being sick as he faces the loss of his lover. When a passing cowboy looks at him, Ennis reasserts his maleness by the violent aggression of his hurled defiance: 'What the fuck are you lookin' at?' Later, his frustration erupts at an Independence Day firework celebration where two men are talking about 'pussy' within the hearing of his young daughters. The aftermath of his violence is shown for the audience's contemplation in a low-angle shot of Ennis with rockets exploding in the sky behind him. The intensity of the bipolar opposites contained in the cultural oxymoron 'gay cowboy' are ever-present beneath Ennis's surface presentation of self. After Alma has observed him kissing Jack, there is a shot of her face as she attempts to come to terms with what she has seen. To her left is Ennis's cowboy hat hanging on a peg on the wall: her struggle is to square this kiss with all that the hat stands for in cultural terms. For Ennis's part, he knows he cannot change the society in which he lives: 'If you can't fix it, Jack, you gotta stand it,' he says. As Harry Benshoff suggests in 'A Straight Cowboy Movie: Heterosexuality According to *Brokeback Mountain*' (2009: 241–242):

> *Brokeback Mountain* represents straight identity as a socially constructed role and speaks of the pressures placed on individuals to reenact such roles constantly. *Brokeback Mountain* is not a gay movie, nor is it a straight movie. It is a queer movie that attempts to unravel the various interlocking traits that comprise contemporary heteronormative identities and institutions.[45]

Figure 4.9   Alma and Ennis's hat (*Brokeback Mountain*, 2005)

This Western took on myths of the 'frontier' that had so far been unchallenged by Hollywood and exposed something of the truth behind them. When Ennis visits Jack's parents after his death, the audience is confronted by the bleak reality and low horizons of Western rural life. The toy cowboy on a horse that Ennis finds in Jack's childhood bedroom embodies the myth of the West while all around is the bland monotony of existence on a small homestead. Throughout the film, Ennis is heroic in the way in which he endures, but it is the heroism of a stoic, steadfast determination to carry on rather than the confident confrontation of wrongs and assertion of rights more usually expected of the Western hero. As he breaks down at their last meeting, he blurts out: 'It's because of you, Jack, that I'm like this: nothing and nowhere.' And then, as they embrace in the closeness of a two-shot, he says: 'Can't stand this anymore, Jack,' but he does stand it. He is the typical loner of Westerns but, as such, he is not romanticized. His childhood was lonely, and his adult loneliness is often emphasized. When we first see him, he is alone in the shot. When he receives the news of Jack's death, he is alone in the shot. When he stands outside Jack's parents' house, he is alone and dwarfed against the whiteness of the building. For Ennis, there is no final shoot-out in which good overcomes evil; there is only the ongoing effort to live with memories of the past. Hidden inside the box of the wardrobe (as his memories are in his mind) is Ennis's shrine to Jack (and to their love) – Jack's clothes from their young days on Brokeback Mountain and a picture of the mountain itself.

THE ASSASSINATION OF JESSE JAMES BY THE COWARD, ROBERT FORD

(2007, Warner Brothers/Jesse Films/Scott Free Productions/Plan B/Alberta Film/ Virtual Studios) Director and screenwriter: Andrew Dominik. Cinematographer: Roger Deakins. Editors: Dylan Tichenor and Curtiss Clayton. Music: Nick Cave and Warren Ellis. Cast: Brad Pitt (Jesse James), Casey Affleck (Robert Ford), Sam Shepard (Frank James), Mary-Louise Parker (Zee James), Paul Schneider (Dick Liddil), Jeremy Renner (Wood Hite), Zooey Deschanel (Dorothy Evans), Sam Rockwell (Charley Ford), Garret Dillahunt (Ed Miller).

Jesse James (Brad Pitt) comes into this film with his character already fully formed. He is a legend in his own short lifetime, a bank robber and murderer with a fearsome reputation. There is no exploration of his past and, therefore, no sense of how he came to be the cold, calculating killer who arrives at Ed Miller's (Garret Dillahunt) shack and terrifies him simply by his mere presence.[46] The resulting implication is that people are born as they are, rather than created out of the circumstances of their experience of life. From the evidence of this film, James is a product of nature, not of nurture; he simply is a psychopath, capable of deranged brutality at one moment and gentle tenderness with his children the next.[47] When he briefly cries after having arrived, dressed from head to foot in black, at a small farmstead and then has violently beaten a young teenage boy for information, the audience can see no real explanation as to why. Only if they know something of the biography of the historical figure of Jesse James might viewers link this to a similar experience of his own as a teenager at the hands of Unionist troops during the Civil War. Of course, the filmmakers have made a deliberate choice to focus on the final months of James's life and the emerging relationship in that period with Robert Ford, the person who is to kill him, and there is no reason they are obliged to account for everything that occurs in some simplistic, equation-like way, as this example might suggest. Nor should they be expected to cover all the events of their central character's life, even if that were possible. Nevertheless, filmmaking choices, especially ones so fundamental to the structure of the narrative, have consequences. To ignore causes for the formation of character and to present a personality as confused (and, therefore, confusing) creates a particular experience for the audience.

One question we might ask would be why this particular version of the Jesse James legend with its already fully formed central character emerged in 2008. The film might claim to be examining the psychology of James in his final months in a more in-depth fashion than previous films have attempted. In looking at the relationship of James with Robert Ford (Casey Affleck), it might claim to focus on a previously under-explored aspect of the story. Yet, it is not a definitive exploration of even this small portion of James's life, and interesting alternative perspectives could have formed the cornerstone of the narrative.[48] In the end, the film is merely one more version of a story constantly replayed and reinterpreted in the United States over a period of more than 100 years. Like all of the other written, filmed, and staged versions, this one exists in relation to a particular society that has produced it at a particular moment in its history. Among the things it might be said to reflect is the fascination not simply of contemporary American society but of early twenty-first-century Western society in general, with a certain limited concept of the psychology of 'evil.' In some ways connected to this, there is also a sense of being absorbed with the nature of celebrity and fame. The relationship between the public, the people, or the masses and their idols both in the late nineteenth century and today is at the heart of this film.[49]

In the period in which the film is set, the emerging mass media of newspapers, magazines, and 'dime novels' created a 'star' out of Jesse James.[50] Robert Ford is shown as being fascinated by this legend, collecting books about his hero and storing them, like a child, in a box of 'treasures' beneath his bed.[51] He is the classic newspaper version of the assassin, a 'nobody' who wants desperately to be 'somebody.' As he says: 'I been a nobody all my life: always the baby.' He often talks in 'dime novel' language as if he is living out one of the stories he has read. He starts out, for example, wanting to be Frank James's (Sam Shepard) 'side-kick' so that Frank can assess his 'grit and intelligence.' Later, when Wood Hite is dying, he says, 'He's still suckin' air but I think he's a goner.' After the assassination, Ford recreates the killing as a stage-show and tours the act, with his brother Charley (Sam Rockwell) playing the role of James. He becomes a celebrity himself but one who is soon rejected by the public as in a popular song about Jesse James that denotes Ford as 'that dirty little coward.'

However, as with all films, the interests being explored are at least as much to do with the present as with the past in which the narrative is set. The role of the mass media in society, and the relationship of the public to stardom, has been an ever-present, ever-developing fact of society from the late nineteenth century to the present day. James is played by Brad Pitt, the single A-list star in the cast who as such can never escape being Pitt; however much he may adopt mannerisms and perform the role of being James, he remains Pitt, the star.[52] The thing that he has become, the thing that the public has made him, and the thing that he sought is awesomely bigger than the man. In this film, Pitt/James becomes an amalgam for the audience. When in the film Ford assassinates James, the viewer knows Pitt is not dead; nor can he ever die, anymore than Bogart or Wayne or a host of others can ever die. Similarly, Jesse James cannot be killed because star status accords immortality. The death (as in the legend/star amalgam that was tagged James Dean) is part of the life of the legend. In this context, the associations of James with Christ in the scenes around his death become even more intriguing. Bob Ford is, in this sphere of connotations, Judas Iscariot in his betrayal. James is Christ in his implied acknowledgment of the necessity of his own death.[53] At one stage, as they seek refuge in a church from the rain, James is shown in the background of a shot lighting two candles with a cross between them. Later, not only does he give the gun to Ford that will be used to kill him but just before this he says to Ford, 'You're going to break a lot of hearts,' a sentence that is at least ambiguous and potentially demonstrates foreknowledge. He also claims to 'go on journeys' out of his body. And just before his death, he walks to church with the family on Palm Sunday. The script then shows Ford as obsessed with the need to wash his hands. At the same time, in the ritual slaughter that is his death, James/Pitt is also potentially Kurtz/Brando in *Apocalyse Now*, who has to die at the hands of Captain Willard (Martin Sheen). Standing on ice in the middle of a river, James says to Charley Ford: 'You ever consider suicide?' His death, like that of Kurtz/Brando, is presented as a form of suicide.

Figure 4.10   The camera and mass media storytelling (*The Assassination of Jesse James by the Coward, Robert Ford*, 2007)

As the dead body of James/Pitt rises into the 2008 camera shot, ready for the actor playing the role of the photographer from the 1880s to take his shot of the dead body, the audience is reminded of the role of the camera in mass media storytelling and prompted to consider that we, too, are watching a series of such constructed images. The key property of the cinematic image, Tom Gunning reminds us, is its 'absent presence' (1995: 34), and this is totally appropriate for an exploration of the phenomenon of legendary status and stardom. Stars and legends are most precisely defined as absent presences. Furthermore, we might note how appropriate the use of a narrator's voice is in this respect. On the one hand, it bestows an air of authenticity and documentary authority and, on the other hand, the style of this narrator's voice that we are given is novelistic, even lyrical, announcing itself as an imaginative reconstruction of possibilities. The voice is then straddling the tension between 'fact' and 'fiction' and, as such, embodies the nature of, and the tension within, the concepts of 'the legend' and 'the star.'

A further possibility would be to suggest this film is crucially about the final death of the Western. Jesse James – perhaps the single key legend underpinning the Wild West myth – never was, this film makes clear, in the West; instead he lived among the middle-class businessmen of Kansas City and robbed banks and held up trains in Virginia, North Carolina, Georgia, and Missouri. Jesse James was little more than a small-time hoodlum caught up in the politics of power played out by the railroads and other big business concerns. The possibilities for interpretation are endless. The Jesse James legend is never fixed and finished for all time; it is forever coming into being. Similarly, the film *The Assassination of Jesse James by the Coward, Robert Ford* is also forever coming into being, open to reinvention and reinterpretation, and we are part of that bringing into being. In interpreting the film one way rather than another, rather than enforcing a single interpretation, our interpretation, we are in fact recognizing the film's polysemy, its endless possibilities for meanings.

NOTES

1. For some consideration of the roles of Ford and scriptwriter, Dudley Nichols, in the creative production of *Stagecoach* see Jennifer Smyth's *Reconstructing American Historical Cinema: from Cimarron to Citizen Kane* (2006: 115–127).
2. Joseph McBride (2003: 288) records six further films in which Monument Valley served as 'the director's dream landscape of the American past' – *My Darling Clementine, Fort Apache, She Wore a Yellow Ribbon, The Searchers, Sergeant Rutledge*, and *Cheyenne Autumn*.
3. The same film also has a shot from a cave mouth as the character played by Wayne is ambushed that is reminiscent of a camera set-up (character framed in doorway) that becomes a trademark of Ford's style. The cinematographer on this film, Archie Stout, was responsible for the photography on many B-Westerns from the period.
4. 'Ford…created in *Stagecoach* a singular prewar Western with one foot planted in U.S. history and the other in American mythology,' (Schatz, 2003: 42).
5. The script, through the words of 'Doc' Boone, makes clear the nature of the settled townships of America. As he and Dallas are driven from the first town, he tells her: 'We're the victims of a foul disease called social prejudice, my child.' And, as Ringo and Dallas leave Lordsburg, the irony in his words has never been more caustic: 'Well, they at least are saved the blessings of civilization.'
6. '*Stagecoach* has more interior scenes than any other Westerns of the period, and Ford used those interiors to reinforce the film's main theme: the besieged condition of civilization,' (Roberts and Olson, 1997: 160).
7. See Nick Browne's 'The Spectator-in-the-Text: The Rhetoric of *Stagecoach*' (Mast, Cohen, and Braudy, 1992: 210–225).
8. Yet, we should also note how Ford refuses to fully condemn any character in a simplistic way (apart, perhaps, from the banker Gatewood). The single

most disturbing shot in the film shows Hatfield, who is standing, taking off his coat before the camera tilts down to the slumped figure of a dead woman whom Hatfield covers with his coat.

9. Does this offer a reflection on the state of the American nation in the late 1930s (and into the early 1940s) when the debate is raging as to whether the country should become involved in the Second World War?

10. This location becomes significant even in its absence in *The Man Who Shot Liberty Valance* (1962).

11. Mark Bould lists nine postwar Westerns that have been described as 'noir Westerns' but suggests there are many more that 'like some scenes in *My Darling Clementine*' employ 'noirish lighting' (2005: 4).

12. This cinematic lighting is in contradiction to the way in which particular efforts have been made within the narrative to place extra lamps above the makeshift operating table.

13. At this point, Ford has Fonda as Wyatt climb over a fence to go to look at the body; the camera naturally tilts up to follow his progress but then momentarily holds a shot of the sky. The end of this tilting shot in a sense adds nothing and could be edited, but its very emptiness or 'nothingness' is a further example of what Lindsay Anderson has labeled the poetry of Ford's work.

> I knew of course that poetry could not be defined. But something impelled me to try. So I began to have some glimmerings of what is, after all, the essence of cinema: the language of style (1981: 14).

14. Peter Wollen mentions in passing in 'The Auteur Theory: Michael Curtiz and *Casablanca*' (Gerstner and Staiger, 2003: 66) that it is the presence of Doc in *My Darling Clementine* that pushes the film toward film noir, but it is surely at least as much down to the presence of Wyatt.

15. When we see Wyatt playing poker, he has in his hand 'three of a kind.' What does this mean? Does it have an attaching symbolism? (Hatfield and Luke Plummer, who both die in *Stagecoach*, both draw the ace of spades.) Who are 'three of a kind'? Wyatt, Doc, and Old Man Clanton? Corey Creekmur suggests the usefulness of seeing these three 'as simply opposed' should be questioned. They are, he says, 'better understood to represent positions of a continuum of social definitions of masculinity' (1995: 171).

16. Old Man Clanton may be killed in the end, but Wyatt's final words to him are ones that banish him from the civilized space of the town: 'get outta town – start wanderin.'

17. '*Shane* is the classic of the classic Westerns' (Wright, 1975: 34). John Saunders (2006: 13) says it is 'often remembered as the archetypal western, a self-conscious attempt to reproduce the familiar themes and characters in a classically pure state,' but he goes on to argue that the film lacks the necessary complexity and depth to be termed a 'classic.'

18. For a more complex reading of point of view in *Shane*, see Patrick McGee's *From Shane to Kill Bill: Rethinking the Western* (2007: 3–5).

19. The pause before using his name is crucial. This naming is entirely different from, and deliberately placed in contrast to, the way in which Marian expresses her next word. It is the same word, 'Shane' but said in an entirely different way.

20. The shock felt by the audience is compounded by the fact that although Wilson easily beats Torrey to the draw, he does not immediately shoot him. Wilson makes Torrey wait for the shot, as the filmmakers force us to await the same thing. In fact, we wait so long that we begin to believe that perhaps it will never come and that maybe, for Wilson, this has been no more than a chance to demonstrate his abilities.

21. Filmed in 1951, the film was not released until 1953, to some extent because of the extensive editing and re-editing undertaken by the director.

22. It is not, as Saunders (2006: 30) suggests, 'difficult to feel' that this is 'expressing the subconscious rivalry' between the two men. Joe has just told Marian how he has seen the 'relationship' between her and Shane: 'I know I'm kinda slow sometimes, Marian, but I see things and I know that if anything happened to me you'd be took care of; took care of better than I could do it myself.' This is language that is controlled and suppresses emotion in a way that is symptomatic of the film as a whole. Furthermore, at the Independence Day celebrations when Shane dances with Marian, the same suppression (or repression) of emotion takes place. They move in a highly formal style that expresses Shane's interest in Marian (see his looks toward her) but maintains their required social detachment from each other. And, as this is happening, the audience is shown Joe observing their ritualistic expression of a growing attachment.

23. Stevens saw this as his 'war film':

> In some sense, Shane is a boy called to go into the Marine Corps because he's the strongest and best qualified to carry out his country's point of view. When you ask a man to fight and to take a life, you not only ask him to risk his own life but you ask him to make a great sacrifice of his moral ideals (quoted in Moss, 2004: 180).

24. Jennifer Wallace, for example, interestingly placing *The Good, the Bad, and the Ugly* within a wider genre context of tragedy, sees Leone's trilogy that culminates in this film as tracing 'a growing scepticism ... about the traditional values upon which pioneering American society depends' (2007: 175).

25. For a detailed look at 'spaghetti westerns,' see Howard Hughes's *Once Upon a Time in the Italian West: the Filmgoers' Guide to Spaghetti Westerns* (2006).

26. This is not entirely new, though: for example, something similar happens in *My Darling Clementine* in the final shoot-out when a stagecoach causes a dust cloud and returns the advantage to Wyatt Earp (Henry Fonda).

27. This is especially so if we have also thought of *Breathless* (1959) and the way in which Jean-Luc Godard references the same moment in Fuller's film by producing a supposed shot along a tube formed from a rolled-up poster.

28. 'Any suggestion that out of the Italian Western formula may have emerged a form of 'critical cinema' is reading too much into a genre which continued

to operate from well within the consensus,' (Frayling, 1981: xv). Mark Poster, conversely, suggests because this film upsets 'the clear delineation of good and evil' (not least by destabilizing the binary opposition of 'good' and 'bad' by the addition of 'ugly'), it 'sets cinema in opposition to mainstream American values as it upsets the moral framework of the Western movie genre' (2006: 139).

29. 'Because Leone's movies differ from some of the other spaghettis in that his do not offer an overt oppositional politics, their reception is in a sense tolerated and even exploited' (Smith, 1993: 17).

30. Although both 'fantastic' and 'stuff' have long recorded etymologies, the use of the phrase 'fantastic stuff' in the sense of 'wonderful material' would seem to have more modern twentieth-century origins. Its use here may be the outcome of Altman's concern to allow actors to develop their parts on set, improvising and embellishing lines according to their interpretation of the nature of their character.

31. Talking about a specific scene that invites two possible interpretations but discussing a general tendency in the film, James Bernardoni says: 'Altman again … insists on neither interpretation, both of which are embedded in a mise-en-scene that respects the complexity of reality,' (2001: 154–155).

32 Feminist issues about the place of women in society are obviously raised here but are left as questions rather than being more fully explored. Talking to Ida, Mrs. Miller says regarding work in the brothel, 'See, the thing is it don't mean nothing.' Leaving aside the fact that this is an ambiguous statement, we might (in terms of the issue) want to see this as the start of a discussion rather than a conclusion.

33. 'Flashing': very slightly exposing the film to soften the images.

34. 'The coarseness was an inextricable part of the fabric, since his intention was not to portray the peasants in their Sunday best … but in their "roughness", in order "to emphasize that those people eating potatoes in the lamplight, have dug the earth with those very hands they put in the dish, and so it speaks of manual labour, and how they have honestly earned their food"' (Hamilton, 1983: 96).

35. '… the country is reduced to the scale of San Francisco, and Dirty Harry roams the city, defying the bureaucracy and restoring order' (Vinocur, 1985: 16).

36. Settlers in these areas often built houses from sods of earth, creating walls up to three feet thick and placing sods on a wooden frame to form the roof. Usually there would be just one door and one window (Hine and Faragher, 2007: 138). See Marianne Bell's Frontier Family Life: A Photographic Chronicle of the Old West (1998: 2) for an image of a 'soddy' – 'The Ira Watson family of Sargent, Nebraska in 1886.'

37. The approach is much like that of the hero in the opening to Shane, but Munny is about to destroy this family rather than defending it like Shane, a fact that Sally instinctively anticipates. The final look between Ned and Sally as he leaves with Munny is perhaps the deepest, most profound moment in the film, conveying an entire relationship without any need for words.

38. See, Bell (1998: 32) – 'The founders of the Shores family, seen here in 1887, went west after the Civil War to start a new life on the Nebraskan plains. Like most former slaves they took the surname of their previous owners.'
39. Logan's Spencer rifle was produced throughout the 1860s but is 10 years out of date by the time he sets out with Munny to pursue the well-known gangster genre premise of 'one final job.'
40. As, maybe, the overuse of negatives in his sentence suggests.
41. If this is the case, it is not a matter of to whom the title refers to; rather, we are all 'unforgiven' because there is no forgiveness to be had.
42. Raphaelle Moine sees the historical period explored by the Western as being 1840–1890 (2008: 13).
43. Christine Geraghty suggests the production team wished to resist association with the Western genre tag but largely it seems because 'the western is no longer a popular film genre' (2008: 153).
44. A key part of farming in the northern states of the mid-West but neglected in Hollywood representations of cowboy agriculture.
45. And not just 'contemporary heteronormative identities and institutions' we might add with an eye on the historic American West.
46. After they have talked, James puts on his black hat, revealing his black glove in the process and, in a single simple movement within one shot, the audience know Miller's fate is sealed. Visual confirmation of Miller's death is delayed until a later flashback when James in the darkness of night shoots his victim in the back and then tenderly comforts his horse that has been startled by the gun fire.
47. 'Although we never really come to know him, Pitt's performance suggests that Jesse is an enigma even to himself' (Horsley, 2009: 184).
48. The almost cameo part in the story played by Frank James (Sam Shepard) offers a clear example of another key relationship that might have been used as a focal point. Similarly, a view from Zee James's (Mary-Louise Parker) perspective would offer fascinating possibilities.
49. There is also, of course, a pattern of political assassinations in U. S. history affecting presidents such as Lincoln, Garfield and Kennedy but also political figures such as Martin Luther King. The concept of 'assassination' is, therefore, a potent term within American culture.
50. 'Jesse James began paying attention to his press clippings in the 1870s, and effectively manipulated the editorial pages of the Kansas City papers. And that is how Bob Ford first learned about him and later became obsessed by him' (Morris, 1995: 145).
51. The theme of Robert Ford as a child is followed in further scenes. In one, he is teased over his box of memorabilia and ends in tears on the ground replacing items in the container with his voice becoming ever more high-pitched. In another, he sits on the ground playing with a child's toy as he talks to James, who sits on a chaise lounge behind him like a father.
52. 'Brad Pitt's fans went to the movie already knowing a great deal about Pitt and his persona. They were familiar with details of his romantic

relationships with Gwyneth Paltrow, Jennifer Aniston, and Angelina Jolie; they knew that he has taken an active role in humanitarian causes like the rebuilding of New Orleans after Hurricane Katrina' (Sikov, 2009: 137).

53. 'You think it's all yarns and newspaper stories, don't you,' says Charley Ford to his brother, Bob. To which Bob replies, 'He's just a human being.'

5

CONCLUSIONS

One further avenue of exploration, much used in other books on the Western but not directly employed here, is to view Westerns in terms of sub-genres. These might include the epic Western, the noir Western, the comedy Western, the spaghetti Western, and the revisionist Western. The contention is that although an overarching genre may exist, it is better seen as being composed of a series of sub-sets. The effort is to take account not only of the fact that films exist within changing social and historical contexts that impact on the evolving nature of a genre but of the reality of a viewing experience in which genres continually overlap and sometimes form particularly potent expressive combinations sufficiently distinctive to be designated as film types in their own right. The implication is that it is, crucially, the changing contexts within which a genre exists and the potential for potent combinations of film types that need to be addressed if the expression of genre to be found in any particular film is to be understood. And who could argue with that. Revisionist Westerns exist as a result of a particular period's utilization of the genre for re-evaluation of the historical reality of the American West. Comedy Westerns fuse the iconographic features of Westerns with a keynote comedic outlook. But how far do we go in this process? Which sub-categories do we accept, which do we reject, and why? Would we wish to further subdivide revisionist Westerns? Certainly we would probably wish to subdivide comedy Westerns, but how far does this take us? Ed Buscombe, worrying about something slightly different – a use of what are seen as different archetypal plot structures to define the Western – feared 'ending up not with one genre called "the western", but an almost infinite number of sub-genres' (2003: 14).

This is an understandable concern as, in the final analysis, the core feature of the concept of genre is its fluidity. Bordwell and Thompson have said, 'The flexibility of genre definitions is shown by the ability of genres to crossbreed freely' (1993: 81). However, here the term *fluidity* is used deliberately as something that goes beyond 'flexibility.' Jeff Collins, following Derrida, suggests texts do not 'belong' to a genre (2006: 57):

> In Derrida's terms, there is no belonging of a text to a genre, no replete membership, but rather the ambiguous condition of participation: belonging in the manner of not belonging.

When approaching the Western, the application of an inter-textual approach – seeing one film against the backdrop of a series of others – would seem to be important as each genre film exists in relation to every other in a system of similarities but, also and more essentially, in a system of differences.[1] Highlighting the importance of this concept of inter-textuality encourages us to continue to carefully consider the relationships between specific aspects of individual texts, and involving ourselves in this detailed process of comparing texts presents us with the impossibility of considering genre outside of socio-historical contexts.

A genre such as the Western can be seen as a means of making sense of aspects of human experience that are difficult to understand and as a way of imposing some form of ordered understanding on complicated periods in social history. Perceived 'dangers' could be said to be tamed by the carefully imposed narrative structures of particular genres. Westerns examine a period of American history involving the westward expansion of empire. They give shape and order to a chaotic historical period in a way that is acceptable to contemporary society. The Western has developed changing thematic concerns over time, but also the same themes have been explored in different ways, in response to changing social perspectives within the wider society. Adding further to the complexity of the mix, different filmmakers have used the same genre to present different positions on the same issues. Then again, a genre might be considered not only as a means of a society explaining itself to itself but as a means of a society's explaining itself to others. Certainly, Hollywood Westerns have been, and will continue to be, exported as products to other countries. In these other places, they have been consumed and, in the process, have given some complex presentation of the United States to the world. Over the years, through the genre of the Western, messages and meanings have been given out and attitudes towards the United States created. As usual, we do have to be wary of oversimplification. As Barry Langford says (2005: 20):

> Claims that the Western or the musical articulate dominant or foundational paradigms for American national identity also need to take account of the presence within the same industry at the same time of genre films that seem directly to challenge those values: film noir, for example.

Going further than this, we might point out that the 'dominant or foundational paradigms for American national identity' will be contested not only between genres, as this quote suggests, but within a genre such as the Western. The representation of the United States to be found in *The Alamo* is very different from that to be found in *Buffalo Bill and the Indians, or Sitting Bull's History Lesson*.

Although there may be broad similarities of thematic structure, plot, and iconography between films produced during different historical periods – without which it would be impossible to conceive of a Western genre – there will also be marked differences. There will be a closer linkage of themes and appearance between films made around the same time, but strong differences will still exist, and contesting ideologies will be at work. A complex picture emerges and, yet, genres such as the Western clearly do change or evolve in response to the historical moment, and without an awareness of social, historical, and political contexts, any interpretation of the significance of these films is impossible.

Genre can be seen as working to affirm cultural values shared by those producing a film and those forming the audience. From this perspective, genre operates to ritually confirm a given understanding of the world by asserting certain consensual social values and norms. John G. Cawelti sees this as offering a partial understanding of the popular Western: 'A ritual is a means of reaffirming certain basic cultural values, resolving tensions and establishing a sense of continuity between present and past,' (1997: 95). From this perspective, Westerns have a social function, reminding an audience of shared values and outlooks and reconfirming its agreement to those values and outlooks. This suggests the producers of films and the audiences for films come together to reconfirm their agreed perspective on the world. However, the same process could also be seen not as embracing the audience in a shared, mutually agreed unity but as manipulating the audience into accepting a dominant social view favoured by an elite group. From this perspective, the audience is not agreeing to this filmic formulation of shared group beliefs but being positioned as victims of disguised social engineering. This view sees the escapism offered by film as manipulation with the gender, race, and class stereotypes of genre limiting the possibilities of how members of the audience might see themselves and reinforcing social norms and values. At the end of a Western with a powerful female central character, such as *Forty Guns* or *Johnny Guitar*, the woman is usually tamed by the man, reduced to symbolic submission to the male. But, then again, maybe the audience cannot be forced into a similar submission; perhaps, in the example given here, for instance, for the female viewer, the reassertion of male control is not enough to cancel out the attractive image of a powerful emancipated woman shown throughout the rest of the film, and it is this that they take away with them as they leave the cinema.

In the final analysis, the approaches to films offered throughout this book remain no more than suggestive of possibilities that are open for you to explore. Every society rewrites its history through its cultural artefacts, but no society has rewritten any period of its history any more thoroughly or continuously over an extended period than the United States has done with the late nineteenth-century history of the American West. Equally, as viewers we are able to shape and reshape our understanding of any film, to examine and re-examine, to interrogate and question, past readings. In the process, we may develop new understandings and new ways of seeing.

NOTE

1. It may be the case that the use of the word *system* here, with its implication of a clearly visible structure, fails to capture the rhizome-like nature of genres.

SIGNIFICANT EVENTS FOR THE WESTERN GENRE

1775–1783
American War of Independence (The American Revolution): British forces are eventually decisively defeated at Yorktown in 1781. Britain formally recognizes American independence (1783) and cedes all land east of the Mississippi.

1776
Declaration of Independence: signed by all thirteen colonies on the eastern seaboard. ['We hold these truths to be self evident, that all men are created equal, that they are endowed by their Creator with certain unalienable rights, that among these, are Life, Liberty, and the pursuit of Happiness.']

1788
American Constitution: ratified, establishing the United States of America. Bill of Rights is added to the Constitution in 1791.

1803
Louisiana Purchase: a huge tract of land stretching from Canada to the Gulf of Mexico between the Rockies and the Mississippi is bought from France.

1804

Meriwether Lewis and William Clark: lead a two-year expedition from the Missouri to the Pacific.

1808

U. S. slave trade is ended: slavery continues with around 4.5 million slaves in the country by 1860.

1812–1815

War with Britain: a major victory is won by the Americans at the Battle of New Orleans, and Native American tribes around the Great Lakes and in the South are effectively defeated.

1823

President James Monroe outlines a foreign policy that becomes known as the 'Monroe Doctrine': European countries should not be allowed new colonies in the region nor should they be able to intervene in the region in such a way as to endanger any nation's independence.

1831–1838

The Trail of Tears: the 'Five Civilized Nations' are forced to leave their tribal lands in the South for a designated Indian Territory west of the Mississippi. The Choctaw, Seminole, Creek, Chickasaw, and Cherokee are all moved, with thousands dying along the way.

1836

Ralph Waldo Emerson's essay *Nature* is published. His writings urge the individual to avoid conformity and affirm that men can intuitively discern God-given truth and then govern themselves according to it.

1836

American settlers in Texas, where they heavily outnumber the Spanish-speaking population, proclaim a republic. The Mexican dictator Santa Anna moves north and wipes out a small American Texan force at the Alamo in

San Antonio but is defeated by the main Texan army at San Jacinto. The independent Texas Republic is recognized by the United States.

1843–1868

An estimated 400,000 people move west in wagon trains along the 2,000-mile Oregon Trail, some going to Oregon and others splitting off to follow further trails to California and Utah.

1845

Cora Montgomery writes an essay 'Annexation' in *The Democratic Review*, suggesting it is the fulfilment of America's 'Manifest Destiny' to 'overspread the continent allocated by Providence for the free development of our yearly multiplying millions.'

After much debate, Texas is annexed to the Union: as a slave state, its admission is favored by some but opposed by others.

1846

Oregon is ceded by Britain to the United States.

1846–1848

Mexican-American War: reports of atrocities during the invasion of Mexico. The border is established at the Rio Grande. Present-day California, Nevada, and Utah, with parts of Colorado, Arizona, New Mexico, and Wyoming, are acquired by the United States.

1847

Sam Colt founds a company in Hartford, Connecticut producing revolvers.

1849

California Gold Rush: by 1850, most surface gold had gone. Later strikes in Idaho, New Mexico, Arizona, Oregon, Montana, Colorado, and Nevada bring further 'gold rushes.'

1850

Donation Land Act: offered 160 acres in Oregon to single men and 320 acres to married couples.

1851

Fort Laramie Treaty: chiefs of the Lakota, Cheyenne, Arapaho, Shoshone, and others guarantee the safety of those on the Oregon Trail and agree to forts being built in exchange for a halt to further settlement on Indian lands.

1857

Butterfield Overland Mail Trail established via Apache Pass: 24 days from St Louis to San Francisco.

1860

With 150 stations 15 miles apart, the Pony Express cuts the mail time to San Francisco to 10 days.

Malaeska: The Indian Wife of the White Hunter, a magazine serial by Ann S. Stephens, published as a dime novel: heyday of dime novels follows and continues until end of First World War.

1861

First transcontinental telegraph line is established.

Westward the Course of Empire Takes Its Way (*Westward Ho!*): a painting by Emanuel Leutze.

1862

Wells Fargo overland stage is established using a route via Fort Laramie and Salt Lake City.

Homestead Act: individuals able to apply for ownership of 160 acres of undeveloped land after five years' residence; adequate acreage in only few places in the West. Staking a claim around a water source becomes critical.

Pacific Railway Act: land and government money is given to the Union Pacific Railroad and Central Pacific Railroad to build a transcontinental railway. The railroad companies end up with millions of acres of public land.

1861–1865
American Civil War: more than 600,000 die as battle casualties or from illness, and hundreds of thousands are maimed. War stimulates industrial growth, urbanization, and demand for wheat and beef.

1861–1864
Cheyenne-Arapaho wars: including the massacre of a Cheyenne settlement at Sand Creek in Colorado.

1862–1868
Sioux Wars: estimates of several hundred white settlers killed in the first year.

1866
Captain William Fetterman and a detachment of 80 troops are killed by Sioux and Cheyenne under Red Cloud in Montana Territory.
Slavery abolished throughout the United States. Ku Klux Klan, an organization of Confederate veterans, inaugurated in Tennessee.
Winchester repeating rifle begins manufacture.

Late 1860s
Texan cattle ranchers begin driving longhorn herds north to railheads. There are four main trails: the Chisholm to Abilene, the Western to Dodge City, the Sedalia to Missouri, and the Goodnight-Loving to Cheyenne.

1869
Transcontinental railway completed: the Central Pacific railroad east from Sacramento (built using a largely Chinese workforce) meets up with the Union Pacific line (built in the main by Irish labourers) coming west from Missouri in Utah. Other lines across the plains follow: the Santa Fe, the Southern Pacific, the Northern Pacific, and the Great Northern.
Ned Buntline's *Buffalo Bill, the King of the Border Men* is published, turned into a stage play three years later.

1870

The Luck of the Roaring Camp and Other Sketches: collection of short stories by Bret Harte.

Newspaper editor Horace Greele, uses what becomes a catch-phrase, 'Go West, young man.'

Early 1870s

Hunters killing around two million buffalo a year; by 1885, the herds have been decimated.

1872

American Progress: painting by John Gast; Columbia as a personification of the United States and a divine-like presence oversees the movement West of pioneers and settlers.

1873

Barbed wire begins to be manufactured; open range increasingly fenced by homesteaders.

1876

Last large-scale 'gold rush': the Black Hills in South Dakota.

1876–1877

Great Sioux War: Lt. Col. George Armstrong Custer defeated by Lakota and Cheyenne forces under Sitting Bull at Little Big Horn.

1878

'Lincoln County War': a struggle over the control of business interests in this area of New Mexico resulting in more than 20 deaths; it is only finally ended when Pat Garrett is appointed county sheriff in 1880 and tracks down and kills Billy the Kid.

1881

'Gunfight at the OK Corral': part of a power struggle between local businessmen and cattlemen.

1883

'Buffalo Bill's Wild West' founded as a touring show: the West is presented through a series of re-enactments highlighting events such as Pony Express riding, Indian attacks on wagon trains, and 'Custer's Last Stand.'

1887

Dawes Act: Indian families offered 160 acres of farmland or 320 acres of grazing land, dividing reservations into privately owned parcels of land.

1889

Oklahoma 'land rush': two million acres in former Indian territory made available for people to stake a claim; more 'land rushes' followed.

Late 1880s

Era of the cattle drive effectively over: fencing of the range, the spread of railroads, and new methods of intensive stock rearing make it no longer economically viable.

1890

Ghost Dance Uprising: troops move into North Dakota, and Sitting Bull is killed while being arrested by Lakota police on Standing Rock Reservation, South Dakota. Chief Big Foot with his Lakota (Sioux) followers is taken to Wounded Knee, South Dakota where 250 men, women, and children are massacred by U. S. Cavalry.

Census Bureau declares the concept of the 'frontier of settlement' is no longer valid: The continent west to the Pacific has been settled.

1892

'Johnson County War': a violent struggle between open-range cattlemen and small homesteaders in the Powder River area of Wyoming.

1893

World's Columbian Exposition in Chicago celebrating the 400th anniversary of the 'discovery' of America: attended by more than 27 million people in six months. Frederick Jackson presents a seminal essay on 'The Significance of the Frontier in American History.'

Thomas Edison's first film production studio is completed at New Jersey.

1894

Sioux Ghost Dance (Edison Manufacturing Company).

1895

American Mutoscope (later Biograph) founded in New Jersey: a prolific film production company through to First World War.

1898

Spanish-American War: United States acquires Puerto Rico, Guam, the Philippines, and effective control of Cuba. It also acquires the Hawaiian Islands.

1899

Cripple Creek Bar-Room Scene (Edison Company).

1902

The Virginian: novel by Owen Wister; fictionalizes the 'Johnson County War' showing lynching as a necessary part of 'frontier justice.'

1903

The Great Train Robbery (Edwin S. Porter, Edison).
Fight for the Water Hole: painting by Frederic Remington.

1907

First volume of Edward S. Curtis's photographic record, *The North American Indian*, published.

Downing the Nigh Leader: Frederic Remington; portrays an Indian attack on stagecoach.

1909
Ford Motor Company begins production of the Model T.

1912
Riders of the Purple Sage: Zane Grey's most famous novel, one of the earliest of more than 40 Westerns he published before the Second World War.

1914
Panama Canal opened through Panama, an 'independent' state under American protection.

1915
The Birth of a Nation (D. W. Griffith): Ku Klux Klan claims four million members by 1924.

1917
United States enters First World War after Germany attacks neutral shipping, with 125,000 casualties in just six months.

1919
Treaty of Versailles ends First World War: Woodrow Wilson dominates peace negotiations advocating free trade and freedom of the seas.
Western Story Magazine started as biweekly: became weekly by end of following year (circulation, two million by 1922). The magazine format effectively replaces the dime novel. Competitor magazines emerge: *Action Stories*, *Lariat Story Magazine*, *Argosy*, *The Frontier*.

1920
Nineteenth Amendment to the U. S. Constitution gives votes to women.

1924

The Iron Horse (John Ford, Fox).

1925

President Calvin Coolidge says, 'The chief business of the American people is business.'

1929

Wall Street Crash: the biggest panic is on 24 October, with 16 million shares being sold.

1930

The Big Trail (Raoul Walsh, Fox).

1932

National Bureau of Economic Research suggests stock market prices down more than 80 percent and more than 15 million unemployed.

Democrat Franklin D. Roosevelt elected: his 'New Deal' employs unprecedented government intervention to help United States out of economic depression. 'We seek to guarantee the survival of free enterprise by guaranteeing conditions under which it can work.'

1933

National Industrial Recovery Act: workers able to organize and bargain collectively 'without interference, coercion, or restraint by employers'; ruled unconstitutional in 1935.

National Labor Board created to mediate in industrial disputes; by 1937, it had arbitrated on 2,000 strikes.

Early 1930s

The 'Dust Bowl': dust storms cause severe damage to agriculture on the prairies. Thousands migrate west in search of work.

1936

American Liberty League formed by businessmen opposing 'the Red New Deal with a Soviet seal.'

1939

Second World War begins, but United States pursues isolationist foreign policy.

Stagecoach (John Ford, United Artists/Walter Wanger Productions).

1941

'Lend-Lease' scheme approved after much debate, enables arms to be supplied to Britain (and Russia) and paid for later.

Japan bombs Pearl Harbor in Hawaii, bringing United States into the war.

They Died With Their Boots On (Raoul Walsh, Warner Brothers).

1944

D-Day landings take place in northern France.

1945

Atomic bombs are dropped on Hiroshima and Nagasaki.

1946

My Darling Clementine (Ford, 20th Century Fox).

Duel in the Sun (King Vidor, Vanguard Films/Selznick Studio).

1947

Truman Doctrine promises help for countries threatened by communism.

Marshall Plan is set up to assist the recovery of West European economies.

House Un-American Activities Committee hearings include the 'Hollywood Ten.'

1948

Berlin Blockade/Airlift: Soviet Union blocks land access to Berlin, and West responds by massive airlift of supplies.

Fort Apache (Ford, RKO/Argosy Pictures).
Red River (Howard Hawks, United Artists/Monterey Productions).

1949
Soviet Union explodes its first atomic bomb.

1950–1953
Korean War: United States and its allies defend South Korea against North Korea supported by China.

1952
High Noon (Fred Zinnemann, United Artists/Stanley Kramer Productions).

1953
Shane (George Stevens, Paramount).

1954
Racial segregation in U. S. schools is ruled unconstitutional.

1957
State governor attempts to prevent the desegregation of high school in Little Rock, Arkansas.

1959
Rio Bravo (Howard Hawks, Warner Brothers/Armada Productions).

1960
The Alamo (John Wayne, Alamo Company/Batjac Productions).

1961
Berlin Wall is completed. 'Bay of Pigs': attempted U. S.-backed invasion of Cuba.

1962

Cuban Missile Crisis: stand-off between United States and Soviet Union narrowly avoids becoming a nuclear exchange.

1963

President John F. Kennedy is assassinated. Civil Rights Movement organizes 'March on Washington for Jobs and Freedom.'

1964–1975

Vietnam War: more than 46,000 Americans killed and 300,000 wounded.

1964

Civil Rights Act passed, outlawing racial discrimination.
A Fistful of Dollars (Sergio Leone, Constantin Film/Jolly Film/Ocean Films, Italy-Spain-West Germany): first of a series of spaghetti Westerns from the director

1965

Malcolm X assassinated.

1966

Black Power and Black Panthers emerge.

1967

Race riots in well more than 100 U. S. cities.

1968

Martin Luther King assassinated; anti-war protests take place.

1969

My Lai Massacre: more than 300 unarmed civilians killed in village in Vietnam. Woodstock music festival in New York State attracts several hundred thousand young people.
The Wild Bunch (Sam Peckinpah, Warner Brothers/Seven Arts Productions).

True Grit (Henry Hathaway, Paramount).

1970

Four students shot dead at Kent State University during a protest at the U. S. invasion of Cambodia.

1971

McCabe & Mrs. Miller (Robert Altman, David Foster Productions/Warner Brothers).

1974

'Watergate' Scandal: the Democratic Party's campaign headquarters is burgled by a team authorized by Republican Party officials. President Nixon resigns.

Blazing Saddles (Mel Brooks, Crossbow/Warner Brothers).

1975

Indian Self-Determination and Education Assistance Act: some recognition of Native American rights.

1979

More than 50 U. S. officials in American Embassy in Tehran seized as hostages.

1980

Ronald Reagan elected president: stresses family values and adopts a tough anti-Soviet stance.

1982

Unemployment in United States reaches 10 percent, highest level since 1930s.

1983

United States invades Grenada.

1985–1987

Three summit meetings are held between President Ronald Reagan and Soviet leader Mikhail Gorbachev.

1986

Iran-Contra Affair: a secret arms deal is arranged with Iran to secure the release of hostages in Lebanon. Funds from the deal are to be used to support Contra guerillas attempting to undermine an elected left-wing government in Nicaragua.

U. S. air strikes are conducted against Libya as retaliation for its alleged support of terrorism in the Middle East.

1989

Berlin Wall comes down.

United States invades Panama.

1991

First Gulf War follows Iraq's invasion of Kuwait.

1992

U. S. troops sent to Somalia and withdrawn in the following year after marines killed.

Unforgiven (Clint Eastwood, Malpaso Productions/Warner Brothers).

1994

U. S. intervention in Haiti.

2001

September 11 attacks on World Trade Center in New York and Pentagon.

U. S. intervention in Afghanistan produces the fall of the Taliban regime.

Patriot Act gives increased power to state agencies to combat terrorism.

2003

U. S.-led invasion of Iraq.

2005

Brokeback Mountain (Ang Lee, Alberta Film/Focus Features/Good Machine/ Paramount/River Road).

2007

The Assassination of Jesse James by the Coward, Robert Ford (Andrew Dominik, Warner Brothers/Jesse Films/Scott Free Productions/Plan B/Alberta Film/Virtual Studios).

GLOSSARY

Auteur: a concept that emerged in France in the late 1940s and early 1950s, when critics suggested certain directors placed their own distinctive stamp on the films they made. These directors were seen as working at a higher level of creativity than those who were more workmanlike and simply put scenes together without imbuing the results with anything of their own personal vision.

Discourse: shared ways of thinking, acting, talking, and representing the world. Social groups are seen as having their own ways of thinking about particular aspects of society. These ways of thinking are then reflected in the way they talk and act and in the way they represent the world to others. Discourses are recognized as being able to shape people's attitudes, beliefs, and behaviours.

Expressionism: the use of non-realist, abstract, angular shapes and forms and dark shadowy lighting to convey a sense of a state of mind, often of psychological anguish. In film, German Expressionism in the post–First World War period is often seen as the forerunner of film noir in America.

Genre: the division of cultural forms such as film into packaged types. Genre theory suggests each film type has its own iconography: characteristic props, costumes, and settings that act as visual signifiers alerting the audience to the genre of the film they are watching. However, the concept of iconography can also refer to the use of sound signifiers and visual signifiers; these might be musical signifiers (characteristic features of the soundtrack) or verbal signifiers (characteristic features of the dialogue).

Ideology: a system of ideas and values or a set of beliefs. An ideological approach to film is based on the theory that all films put forward a particular view of the world, a way of seeing society and social relations that is essentially political.

Naturalism: the recording of closely observed details of human life. The suggestion is that through close observation and realistic recording of human interaction, it is possible to gain a better understanding of the complexities of both individual characters and the wider society.

Postmodernism/postmodernity: terms used to describe the contemporary period. The postmodern period is said to be characterized by a loss of faith in old meta-narratives, or 'grand narratives,' such as Christianity and Marxism, that were once believed capable of explaining the world. The postmodern world is said to be experienced in terms of discontinuity, fragmentation, and growing individual confusion.

Psychoanalytical film theory: an approach to analyzing the relationship of the spectator to film and a means of exploring relationships between characters in films. Sigmund Freud proposed a hidden dimension to life beneath our experience of surface 'reality.' He suggested we each strive to fulfil our desires, especially sexual desires, while at the same time experiencing guilt for those desires. Jacques Lacan's concept of the 'mirror phase' of childhood development – obtaining an illusion of wholeness by seeing the self out in the world – has been compared to an act of spectatorship in which the viewer identifies with a character on the screen.

Realism: a set of codes and conventions given cultural primacy within photographic representations. The camera can be seen as 'simply' visually recording what is 'out there' in the world, but it is, in fact, no more than another means of representing the world to an audience. The images produced depend on the input of the camera operator and editor. No final, definitive 'reality' can be captured; it is forever elusive and can be given only particular interpretations.

Representation: the way in which reality is depicted in texts and the resulting meanings generated for the audience. Commonly, representations are considered as reflections or distortions of reality. It is often seen as the attribution of certain characteristics to individuals or groups, but places or events are also presented to the viewer in certain chosen ways. Such representations often amount to culturally accepted stereotypes.

Semiotics/semiology: the study of meaning as inscribed within individual 'signs' that are seen to be operating within codes and conventions. C. S. Peirce (d. 1914) suggested there were three types of sign: an 'icon' resembled the object described (a photograph, for example); an 'index' worked through a direct link between sign and object (smoke, for example, indicated something beyond itself, i.e., fire); and a 'symbol' had neither direct resemblance nor direct connection to the object indicated but only an agreed cultural link (a red rose, for example, may be linked to the idea of love). In the 1970s, Roland Barthes suggested a sign had a simple, surface, or literal meaning at the level of 'denotation' and a further potential set of meanings at the level of 'connotation' consisting of the social and cultural associations linked to the sign.

Star theory: stars are a key element in the organization of the film industry operating as a brand name for marketing purposes. In ideological terms, a star could be seen to work to reinforce (or challenge) a society's dominant pattern of attitudes, values and norms. From this perspective, stars can be seen as sites of ideological struggle. Dominant star images and the meanings stars embody for a society will vary from one historical period to another.

FURTHER READING

Buscombe, Edward (2006), *100 Westerns*, London: BFI – includes a plot synopsis, major credits, and a commentary on each film. The introduction considers a series of key concepts in relation to the Western genre. In its compendium-style approach, this amounts to an in-depth book.

Carter, David (2008), *The Western*, Harpenden: Kamera Books – a compendium of films, actors, and directors. This book opens with an evaluation of the historical American West. It then traces the development of the genre in a chronological fashion from silent films to revisionist Westerns.

Coyne, Michael (1998), *The Crowded Prairie: American National Identity in the Hollywood Western*, London and New York: I. B. Tauris – examines Westerns from 1939 to 1976 in relation to American domestic and foreign policy.

French, Philip (2005), *Westerns: Aspects of a Movie Genre and Westerns Revisited*, Manchester: Carcanet – argues that films made in this genre from the end of the Second World War to the mid-1970s can be seen as reflecting the ideologies of four politicians from the period.

Hughes, Howard (2008), *Stagecoach to Tombstone: The Filmgoers' Guide to Great Westerns*, London and New York: I. B. Tauris – in-depth details of film production for a series of Westerns from 1939.

Kitses, Jim (2008), *Horizons West: The Western from John Ford to Clint Eastwood*, (1969) Basingstoke: Palgrave Macmillan – a carefully researched study that is detailed in its auteurist approach. The works of the directors John Ford, Anthony Mann, Budd Boetticher, Sam Peckinpah, Sergio Leone, and Clint Eastwood are considered at length.

Lenihan, John H. (1985), *Showdown: Confronting Modern America in the Western Film*, Champaign, IL: University of Illinois Press – sees the Western as reflecting central social tensions in American society from the 1930s to the 1970s.

Lusted, David (2003), *The Western*, Harlow: Pearson Education – divides the Western into a series of sub-genres from 'silent' Westerns to 'revisionist' Westerns.

McGee, Patrick (2007), *From Shane to Kill Bill: Rethinking the Western*, Malden, MA and Oxford: Blackwell – explores the development of the Western from 1939 to the present with a strong examination of class issues.

McVeigh, Stephen (2007), *The American Western*, Edinburgh: Edinburgh University Press – focuses not only on cinema but on literature and histories of the period covered by Western films.

Saunders, John (2001), *The Western Genre: From Lordsburg to Big Whiskey*, London and New York: Wallflower – considers key issues for the genre such as the concepts of 'Art or entertainment?' and 'History or myth?' before moving, in the first chapter, to a full-scale reading of *Shane* as an exemplar Western.

Simmon, Scott (2003), *The Invention of the Western Film: A Cultural History of the Genre's First Half-Century*, Cambridge: Cambridge University Press – offers thoroughly interesting and challenging academic insights, especially to early Westerns, a period not often covered.

Simpson, Paul (2006), *The Rough Guide to Westerns*, London: Rough Guides – offers easily accessible profiles of actors, directors, and essential films.

Walker, Janet (ed) (2001), *Westerns: Films Through History*, New York and London: Routledge – an academic investigation of the genre's relationship to history and myth.

BIBLIOGRAPHY

Abercrombie, N. (1996). *Television and Society*, Cambridge: Polity Press.

Altman, R. (1999). *Film/Genre*, London: BFI.

American Security Council Foundation Strategy Board, Coalition for Peace Through Strength (1984). *A Strategy for Peace Through Strength*, Ann Arbor, MI: University of Michigan Press.

Anderegg, M. A. (1991). *Inventing Vietnam: The War in Film and Television*, Philadelphia, PA: Temple University Press.

Anderson, L. (1981). *About John Ford*, London: Plexus.

Andreychuk, E. (1997). *The Golden Corral: A Roundup of Magnificent Western Films*, Jefferson, NC: McFarland.

Astruc, A. (1967). 'The Birth of a New Avant-Garde: La Caméra-Stylo,' in P. Graham (ed.), *The New Wave*, Garden City: Doubleday.

Bal, M. and Bryson, N. (1991). 'Semiotics and Art History,' *Art Bulletin* 73 (2): 174, in G. Rose (2007), *Visual Methodologies: An Introduction to the Interpretation of Visual Materials*, London: Sage.

Barra, A. (2009). *Inventing Wyatt Earp: His Life and Many Legends*, Lincoln, NE: University of Nebraska Press.

Barthes, R. (1972 [1957]). *Mythologies*, trans. A. Lavers, London: Cape.

Baudrillard, J. (1983). *Simulations*, New York: Semiotext.

Beard, W. (2000). *Persistence of Double Vision: Essays on Clint Eastwood*, Edmonton: University of Alberta Press.

Bell, M. (1998). *Frontier Family Life: A Photographic Chronicle of the Old West*, New York: Barnes and Noble.

Benshoff, H. M. (2009). 'A Straight Cowboy Movie: Heterosexuality According to *Brokeback Mountain*,' in S. Griffin (ed.), *Hetero: Queering Representations of Straightness*, Albany, NY: State University of New York Press.

Benshoff, H. M. and Griffin, S. (2004). *America on Film: Representing Race, Class, Gender and Sexuality at the Movies*, Malden, MA and Oxford: Wiley-Blackwell.

Bernardoni, J. (2001). *New Hollywood: What the Movies Did With the New Freedoms of the Seventies*, Jefferson, NC: McFarland.

Blake, M. F. (2006). *Hollywood and the OK Corral: Portrayals of the Gunfight and Wyatt Earp*, Jefferson, NC: McFarland.

Bordwell, D. and Thompson, K. (1993). *Film Art: An Introduction*, New York: McGraw-Hill.

Bould, M. (2005). *Film Noir: From Berlin to Sin City*, London: Wallflower.

Brewer, P. R. (2008). *Value War: Public Opinion and the Politics of Gay Rights*, Lanham, MD: Rowman and Littlefield.

Brown, D. (1978). *Hear That Lonesome Whistle Blow*, New York: Bantam.

Browne, N. (1992). 'The Spectator-in-the-Text: The Rhetoric of *Stagecoach*,' in G. Mast, M. Cohen, and L. Braudy (eds), *Film Theory and Criticism: Introductory Readings* (4th edn), New York and Oxford: Oxford University Press.

Buscombe, E. (ed.) (1991). *The BFI Companion to the Western*, London: Museum of the Moving Image.

Buscombe, E. (2003). 'The Idea of Genre in the American Cinema' in B. K. Grant (ed.), *Film Genre Reader III, Volume 3*, Austin, TX: University of Texas.

Casper, D. (2007). *Postwar Hollywood: 1946–1962*, Malden, MA and Oxford: Blackwell.

Cawelti, J. G. (1997). 'The Six-Gun Mystique' in B. Ashley (ed) *Reading Popular Narrative: A Source Book*, London and Washington: Leicester University Press.

Chatman, S. B. (1978). *Story and Discourse: Narrative Structure in Fiction and Film*, Ithaca, NY: Cornell University Press.

Collins, J. (2006). 'The Genericity of Montage: Derrida and Genre Theory' in G. Dowd, L. Stevenson, and J. Strong (eds), *Genre Matters: Essays in Theory and Criticism*, Bristol and Portland, OR: Intellect.

Corkin, S. (2004). *Cowboys as Cold Warriors: the Western and U.S. History*, Philadelphia, PA: Temple University Press.

Creekmur, C. K. (1995). 'Acting Like a Man: Masculine Performance in *My Darling Clementine*' in C. K. Creekmur and A. Doty (eds), *Out in Culture: Gay, Lesbian, and Queer Essays on Popular Culture*, New York: Continuum.

D'haen, T. (1997). 'The Western,' in H. Bertens (ed.), *International Postmodernism: Theory and Literary Practice*, Amsterdam and Philadelphia, PA: John Benjamins.

Dancyger, K. (2007). *The Technique of Film and Video Editing: History, Theory and Practice*, Boston, MA and Oxford: Focal Press.

Dixon, W. W. (ed.) (2006). *American Cinema of the 1940s: Themes and Variations*, Piscataway, NJ: Rutgers University Press.

Dombrowski, L. (2008). *The Films of Sam Fuller: If You Die, I'll Kill You!* Middletown, CT: Wesleyan University Press.

Durham, M. G. and Kellner, D. M. (2006). *Media and Cultural Studies: Key Works*, Malden, MA and Oxford: Blackwell.

Dyer, R. (1985). 'Taking Popular Television Seriously,' in D. Lusted and P. Drummond (eds), *TV and Schooling*, London: BFI.

Dyer, R. (1986). *Heavenly Bodies: Film Stars and Society*, London: Macmillan.

Dyer, R. (2002). *The Matter of Images: Essays on Representation*, London: Routledge.

Egan, J. (1980) 'Bombs Away: Trouble in Hollywood,' *New York Magazine*, December 8: 16

Emerson, R. W. (1903). *Letters and Social Aims*, London and New York: Macmillan.

Etulain, R. W. and Malone, M. P. (2007). *The American West: A Modern History, 1900 to the Present* (2nd edn), Lincoln, NE and London: University of Nebraska Press.

Fiske, J. (1989). *Reading the Popular*, London: Unwin Hyman.

Fiske, J. and Hartley J. (1978). *Reading Television*, London: Methuen.

Flores, R. R. (2002). *Remembering the Alamo: Memory, Modernity and the Master Symbol*, Austin, TX: University of Texas Press.

Frayling, C. (1981). *Spaghetti Westerns: Cowboys and Europeans from Karl May to Sergio Leone*, London: Routledge.

Fujitani, T., White, G. M., and Yoneyama, L. (2001). *Perilous Memories: the Asia-Pacific War(s)*, Durham, NC: Duke University Press.

Fulwood, N. (2003). *One Hundred Violent Films That Changed Cinema*, London: Batsford.

Geraghty, C. (2008). *Now a Major Motion Picture: Film Adaptations of Literature and Drama*, Lanham, MD: Rowman and Littlefield.

Gerstner, D. A. and Staiger, J. (eds) (2003). *Authorship and Film*, New York and London: Routledge.

Gillespie, M. and Toynbee, J. (2006). *Analysing Media Texts*, Milton Keynes: Open University Press.

Grant, B. K. (2007). *Film Genre: From Iconography to Ideology*, London: Wallflower.

Greenberg, A. S. (2005). *Manifest Manhood and the Antebellum American Empire*, Cambridge: Cambridge University Press.

Gunning, T. (1995). 'Those Drawn With a Very Fine Camel's Hair Brush: The Origins of Film Genres,' *Iris* 20: 49–61, quoted in R. Moine (2008), *Cinema Genre*, trans. A. Fox and H. Radner, Oxford and Malden, MA: Blackwell.

Hall, S. (1973). 'The Determination of News Photographs,' in S. Cohen and J. Young (eds), *The Manufacture of News*, London: Constable.

Hall, S. (2006). 'Encoding/Decoding,' in M. G. Durham and D. Kellner (eds), *Media and Cultural Studies: Keyworks*, (2nd edn), Malden, MA and Oxford: Blackwell.

Hallam, J. and Marshment, M. (2000). *Realism and Popular Cinema*, Manchester: Manchester University Press.

Hamilton, G. H. (1983). *Painting and Sculpture in Europe 1880–1940*, (3rd edn), Harmondsworth: Penguin.

Harris, C. W. and Rainey, B. (2002). *The Cowboy: Six-Shooters, Songs and Sex*, Norman, OK: University of Oklahoma Press.

Hine, R. V. and Faragher, J. M. (2007). *Frontiers: A Short History of the American West*, New Haven, CT and London: Yale University Press.

Horsley, J. (2009). *The Secret Life of Movies: Schizophrenic and Shamanic Journeys in America*, Jefferson, NC: McFarland.

Hughes, H. (2006). *Once Upon a Time in the Italian West: The Filmgoers' Guide to Spaghetti Westerns*, London: I. B. Tauris.

Hughes, H. (2008). *Stagecoach to Tombstone: The Filmgoers' Guide to the Great Westerns*, London: I.B. Tauris.

Jenkins, P. (2007). *A History of the United States* (3rd edn), Basingstoke and New York: Palgrave Macmillan.

Jewell, R. B. (2007). *The Golden Age of Cinema: Hollywood, 1929–1945*, Malden, MA and Oxford: Blackwell.

Jorgensen, M. and Phillips, L. J. (2002). *Discourse Analysis as Theory and Method*, London: Sage.

Kilpatrick, J. (1999). *Celluloid Indians: Native Americans and Film*, Lincoln, NE: University of Nebraska.

Kitses, J. (1969). *Horizons West: Anthony Mann, Budd Boetticher, Sam Peckinpah: Studies of Authorship within the Western*, London: Thames and Hudson.

Kuhn, A. (1990). *Alien Zone: Cultural Theory and Contemporary Science Fiction*, London: Verso.

Lackmann, R. W. (1997). *Women of the Western Frontier in Fact, Fiction and Film*, Jefferson, NC: McFarland.

Langford, B. (2005). *Film Genre: Hollywood and Beyond*, Edinburgh: Edinburgh University Press.

Lawton, B. (1994). 'America Through Italian/American Eyes: Dream or Nightmare?' in A. J. Tamburri, P. Giordano, and F. L. Gardaphe (eds), *From the Margins: Writings in Italian Americana* (2nd edn), West Lafayette, IN: Purdue University Press.

Lewis, R. W. (1971). 'John Wayne: The Playboy Interview,' *Playboy Magazine* 18 (5): 77, May 1971.

Linderman, G. F. (1999). *The World within War: America's Combat Experience in World War II*, Cambridge, MA and London: Harvard University Press.

Loy, R. P. (2004). *Westerns in a Changing America, 1955–2000*, Jefferson, NC: McFarland.

Luhr, W. (1996). 'Reception, Representation, and the OK Corral: Shifting Images of Wyatt Earp,' in B. Braendlin and H. P. Braendlin (eds), *Authority and Transgression in Literature and Film*, Gainesville, FL: University Press of Florida.

Lyotard, J.-F. (1984). *The Postmodern Condition*, Manchester: Manchester University Press.

Mainon, D. and Ursini, J. (2006). *Modern Amazons: Warrior Women on Screen*, Milwaukee, WI: Limelight Editions.

Martin, J. D. (1996). '"The Grandest and Most Cosmopolitan Object Teacher": Buffalo Bill's Wild West and the Politics of American Identity, 1883–1899,' Radical History Review, 66, 99–123.

Mayers, D. (2007). Dissenting Voices in America's Rise to Power, Cambridge: Cambridge University Press.

McBride, J. (2004). Searching for John Ford: A Life, London: Faber.

McGee, P. (2007). From Shane to Kill Bill: Rethinking the Western, Malden, MA and Oxford: Blackwell.

McGowan, T. and Kunkle, S. (2004). 'Introduction: Lacanian Psychoanalysis in Film Theory,' in T. McGowan and S. Kunkle (eds), Lacan and Contemporary Film, New York: Other Press.

McLynn, F. (2003). Wagons West: The Epic Story of America's Overland Trails, London: Pimlico.

Metz, C. (1974). Language and Cinema, The Hague: Mouton.

Moine, R. (2008). Cinema Genre, trans. A. Fox and H. Radner, Oxford and Malden, MA: Blackwell.

Morris, G. L. (1995). Talking Up a Storm: Voices of the New West, Lincoln, NE: University of Nebraska Press.

Moss, M. A. (2004). Giant: George Stevens, a Life on Film, Madison, WI: Terrace Books.

Mulvey, L. (2004). 'Afterthoughts on "Visual Pleasure and Narrative Cinema" Inspired by Duel in the Sun (King Vidor, 1946),' in P. Simpson, A. Utterson. and K. J. Shepherdson (eds), Film Theory: Critical Concepts in Media and Cultural Studies, London: Routledge.

Murphy, B. (2003). Congressional Theatre: Dramatizing McCarthyism on Stage, Film and Television, Cambridge: Cambridge University Press.

Murray, J. A. (2000). Cinema Southwest: An Illustrated Guide to the Movies and their Locations, Flagstaff, AZ: Northland Publishing.

Nash, G. D. (1985). The American West Transformed: The Impact of the Second World War, Bloomington, IN: Indiana University Press.

Neale, S. (1980). Genre, London: BFI.

Nelmes, J. (ed.) (2003). An Introduction to Film Studies, (3rd edn) London and New York: Routledge.

Niemi, R. (2006). History in the Media: Film and Television, Santa Barbara, CA: ABC-CLIO.

Nolley, K. (2003). 'The Representation of Conquest: John Ford and the Hollywood Indian, 1939–1964,' in P. C. Rollins and J. E. O'Connor (eds), Hollywood's Indians: The Portrayal of the Native American in Film, Lexington, KT: University Press of Kentucky.

Norman, B. (1991). Talking Pictures: The Story of Hollywood, London: Arrow.

Pearson, R. E. and Simpson, P. (eds) (2001). Critical Dictionary of Film and Television Theory, London: Routledge.

Phillips, G. D. (1999). *Major Film Directors of the American and British Cinema*, (2nd edn), Bethlehem, PA: Lehigh University Press.

Porter, D. (2005). *Howard Hughes: Hell's Angel*, New York: Blood Moon.

Poster, M. (2006). *Information Please: Culture and Politics in the Age of Digital Machines*, Durham, NC: Duke University Press.

Prince, S. (ed.) (1999). *Sam Peckinpah's 'The Wild Bunch,'* Cambridge: Cambridge University Press.

Quart, L. and Auster, A. (1984). *American Film and Society since 1945*, London and Basingstoke: Macmillan.

Rainey, B. (2002). 'The "Reel" Cowboy,' in C. W. Harris and Buck Rainey (eds), *The Cowboy: Six-Shooters, Songs and Sex*, Norman, OK: University of Oklahoma Press.

Rand, Y. (2005). *Wild Open Spaces: Why We Love Westerns*, Manville, RI: Maverick Spirit Press.

Roberts, R. and Olson, J. S. (1997). *John Wayne: American*, Lincoln, NE: University of Nebraska Press.

Robertson, P. (1996). *Guilty Pleasures: Feminist Camp from Mae West to Madonna*, London: I. B. Tauris.

Roosevelt, T. (1896). *The Winning of the West: Louisiana and the Northwest, 1791–1807*, New York and London: G. P. Putnam.

Roosevelt, T. (2006). *The Strenuous Life: Essays and Addresses*, New York: Cosimo.

Rose, G. (2007). *Visual Methodologies: An Introduction to the Interpretation of Visual Material*, London: Sage.

Ryan, M. and Kellner D. (1990). *Camera Politica: The Politics and Ideology of Contemporary Hollywood*, Bloomington, IN: Indiana University Press.

Sarris, A. (2005). 'Auteur Theory and Film Evaluation' *Film Culture* 27 (Winter 1962/63): 1–8, in T. E. Wartenberg and A. Curran (eds), *The Philosophy of Film: Introductory Texts and Readings*, Malden, MA and Oxford: Blackwell.

Saunders, J. (2006). *The Western Genre: From Lordsburg to Big Whiskey*, London: Wallflower.

Schatz, T. (2003). '*Stagecoach* and Hollywood's A-Western Renaissance,' in B. K. Grant (ed.), *John Ford's 'Stagecoach,'* Cambridge: Cambridge University Press.

Schultz, R. (1990). 'Celluloid History: Postwar Society in Postwar Culture,' *American Studies* (Online). Available at: http://journals.ku.edu/index.php/amerstud/article/viewFile/2911/2870 [Accessed 12 May, 2010]

Seydor, P. (1999). *Peckinpah: the Western Films – A Reconsideration*, Champaign, IL: University of Illinois Press.

Shipman, D. (1979). *The Great Movie Stars: The Golden Years*, London: Angus and Robertson.

Sikov, E. (2009). *Film Studies: An Introduction*, New York: Columbia University Press.

Simmon, S. (2003). *The Invention of the Western Film: A Cultural History of the Genre's First Half-Century*, Cambridge: Cambridge University Press.

Simpson, P., Utterson, A., and Shepherdson, K. J. (2004). *Film Theory: Critical Concepts in Media and Cultural Studies*, Volume 3, London: Routledge.

Slotkin, R. (1998). *Gunfighter Nation: the Myth of the Frontier in Twentieth-Century America*, Norman, OK: University of Oklahoma Press.

Smith, A. (2007). 'Soul Wound: The Legacy of Native American Schools,' *Amnesty Magazine* (Online). Available at: http://www.amnestyusa.org/amnestynow/soulwound.html [Accessed 10 May, 2010].

Smith, P. (1993). *Clint Eastwood: A Cultural Production*, Minneapolis, MN: University of Minnesota Press.

Smyth, J. E. (2006). *Reconstructing American Historical Cinema: from Cimarron to Citizen Kane*, Lexington, KY: University Press of Kentucky.

Spencer, K. (2008). *Film and Television Scores 1950–1979: A Critical Survey by Genre*, Jefferson, NC: McFarland.

Stam, R. (2000). 'The Birth of the Spectator,' in R. Stam (ed.), *Film Theory: An Introduction*, Malden, MA and Oxford: Blackwell.

Studlar, G. and Bernstein, M. (2001). *John Ford Made Westerns: Filming the Legend in the Sound Era*, Bloomington, IN: Indiana University Press.

Sultanik, A. (1986). *Film, A Modern Art*, Cranbury, NJ: Cornwall Books.

Thomas, D. (1996). 'John Wayne's Body,' in I. Cameron and D. Pye (eds), *The Movie Book of the Western*, London: Studio Vista.

Thompson, K. and Bordwell, D. (2002). *Film History: An Introduction*, New York: McGraw-Hill.

Thurschwell, P. (2000). *Sigmund Freud*, London: Routledge.

Tindall, G. B. and Shi, D. E. (2007). *America: A Narrative History Volume 2*, (7th edn), New York and London: W.W. Norton.

Turner, G. (1999). *Film as Social Practice*, London: Routledge.

Vinocur, J. (1985). 'Clint Eastwood, Seriously,' *New York Times Magazine*, February 24, 1985.

Wallace, J. (2007). *The Cambridge Introduction to Tragedy*, Cambridge: Cambridge University Press.

Walsh, M. (2005). *The American West: Visions and Revisions*, Cambridge: Cambridge University Press.

Winkler, M. M. (2001). *Classical Myth and Culture in Cinema*, Oxford: Oxford University Press.

Wollen, P. (2003). 'The Auteur Theory: Michael Curtiz and *Casablanca*,' in D. A. Gerstner and J. Staiger (eds), *Authorship and Film*, New York and London: Routledge.

Wood, A. L. (2009). *Lynching and Spectacle: Witnessing Racial Violence in America, 1890–1940*, Chapel Hill, NC: University of North Carolina Press.

Wright, W. (1975). *Six-Guns and Society: A Structural Study of the Western*, Berkeley, CA: University of California Press.

INDEX